D1539363

"Thanks to dramatic technological advances of the past decade, computers can help us become smarter and smarter in our everyday tasks. As a result, today's customers are much more sophisticated, and companies need to change in response. Kasanoff and Hinshaw highlight some of these changes and help companies understand how to deal with smart customers."

— Roberto Pieraccini, author of *THE VOICE IN THE MACHINE: Building Computers That Understand Speech,* and director of the International Computer Science Institute at Berkeley (ICSI)

"This engaging book provides a useful road map for navigating today's and tomorrow's technological innovations to improve your customer's experience. Ignore its lessons at your (and your shareholders') peril."

— Christopher Oddleifson, President & Chief Executive Officer, Rockland Trust Company

"Bruce Kasanoff and Michael Hinshaw have correctly flagged the start of a major revolution. I especially hope their SMART framework gets adopted in education, where we desperately need a new approach."

— Bart Stuck, Managing Director, Signal Lake

"Every CEO should read this book. The bigger your company the more you need a reality check and this book is just that. Your customers now know more than you do about your business and your competition. With so many innovative technologies present today and coming soon, your IT department and marketing team need to work together to elevate your brand awareness and start communicating more effectively with your customers. This is a must read for all business executives!"

— Jocelyn Smith, Managing Partner, CEO, infinitee Communications

SMART CUSTOMERS
STUPID COMPANIES

WHY ONLY INTELLIGENT COMPANIES WILL THRIVE, AND HOW TO BE ONE OF THEM

Business Strategy Press

Requests for permission should be directed to
permissions@businessstrategypress.com
or mailed to Permissions at:

Business Strategy Press
545 Eighth Avenue, Suite 401
New York, NY 10018-4307
www.businessstrategypress.com

Printed in the United States of America
First Edition: May 2012

ISBN 978-0-9851339-1-7

Hinshaw, Michael
Kasanoff, Bruce

Smart Customers Stupid Companies: Why Only Intelligent Companies Will Thrive, and How to Be One of Them

SPECIAL SALES

Business Strategy Press books are available at special discounts for bulk purchases, sales promotions, or premiums. Special editions, including personalized covers, excerpts of existing books, and corporate imprints can be created in quantity for special needs.

For more information, contact Specialty Markets by emailing
specialty@businessstrategypress.com.

"IF YOU DON'T LIKE CHANGE, YOU'RE GOING TO LIKE IRRELEVANCE EVEN LESS."
— GENERAL ERIC SHINSEKI,
RETIRED CHIEF OF STAFF, U. S. ARMY

Contents

THREE: A PERFECT STORM OF DISRUPTIVE INNOVATION

FOUR: STUPID COMPANIES

FIVE: GET SMART

SIX: CRITICAL STEPS

AUTHORS

INDEX

SOURCES

Introduction

WE ARE NOT TALKING ABOUT TRIVIAL CHANGE

Over the past decade...

...portable computers became ubiquitous, then morphed into ever smaller, more powerful, and cheaper phones and tablets...

...painfully slow connections gave way to omnipresent broadband wireless...

...control of information shifted from the media to the forum of public opinion...

...computer programming went from something IT departments did very slowly and mysteriously to something nearly anyone can do...

...it became as cheap, easy, and common to video chat with someone on the other side of the world as to call a friend across town...

...mass production and consumption of news, entertainment, products, services, and ideas have lost the battle, giving way to personalization and customization.

All along the way, successful and even venerable companies have managed to hide their heads in the sand or let inertia and other internal obstacles get the better of them.

Databases of customer information remain in silos, their divisions don't cooperate, employees aren't paid to focus on customer needs, and systems and processes that were never intended to be flexible...well, they remain that way.

Only the most "intelligent" companies will be able to respond to – and profit from – these radically greater customer expectations.

At the same time, everything and everyone has become or is becoming interconnected. Customers have smartphones loaded with apps that let them check prices, compare service agreements, read reviews, and check in with friends (and strangers) even as they examine your offers and products, and those of your competitors.

Consumers and businesses alike research, connect, and purchase online and over their phones without a second thought.

With these tools come radically higher customer expectations. Higher expectations of experience. Greater demands for personalization and customization. Lower tolerance for mistakes, for running through inane hoops, or for interactions that require mindless repetition ("What is your account number?").

In short, the world has changed dramatically, but many companies have not. Forget about innovation, they're not even sure how to keep up.

This is the challenge your company needs to confront.

YOUR CUSTOMERS ARE SMARTER THAN YOU MAY REALIZE

The same disruptive forces driving these changes make it possible for you to radically improve customer experience.

Among the many disruptive forces that are making it impossible for firms to survive with outdated strategies, four in particular are changing the basic ground rules for business competition, and are the focus of this book: Social Influence, Pervasive Memory, Digital Sensors, and the Physical Web.

Did Polaroid see change coming?

"THE NETWORKED ECONOMY KNOWS MORE THAN COMPANIES DO ABOUT THEIR OWN PRODUCTS. AND WHETHER THE NEWS IS GOOD OR BAD, THEY TELL EVERYONE." — THE CLUETRAIN MANIFESTO

- **Social Influence** inserts other people and their opinions between a company and its customers, radically disrupting traditional notions of customer relationship lifecycles.

- **Pervasive Memory** is the data that accumulate in huge volumes as we interact through digital devices. It delivers competitive advantages to firms that leverage this data to benefit customers. Companies that don't collect, analyze, and utilize this data – or that mishandle it – will fail.

- **Digital Sensors** are the trillions of devices that see, hear, and feel what is happening in our world. They bring intelligence to everything that surrounds us. Smart companies must have smart products and services. Sensors are what make products smart, and sensors will change business competition more than computers did.

- **The Physical Web** is emerging, allowing us to browse, bookmark, tag, and manipulate the physical world much as we do on the Web. This shift encompasses the Internet of Things, but goes far beyond it. We're not just linking devices to devices. We are linking people, places, ideas, and things; doing so will change the very definitions of corporations, innovation, and competition.

Together, these forces will bring customers more choices, better information, and stunning new services.

They are already providing individuals with tools more advanced, in many cases, than the most sophisticated commercial enterprises had just five years ago.

Put another way, they'll continue to make your customers even smarter. And they can make your company more intelligent, too.

This book will help you profit from disruptive innovation – rather than falling victim to it.

For reasons that will become crystal clear as you read on, established firms will need to reinvent themselves and disrupt their own industries to stay alive. With thousands upon thousands of very bright developers and entrepreneurs working around the globe to provide your customers with ever better, ever more disruptive tools, it's a certainty that innovation will be coming to your industry if it hasn't already.

Those companies that react slowly or tentatively will be increasingly marginalized, until finally, they'll wither away. It may take 5, 10, or even 15 years, but eventually, these companies will be smothered by the competition and the growing demands of their ever-smarter customers.

We wrote this book to make sure you're not one of them.

Michael Hinshaw
Bruce Kasanoff

May 2012

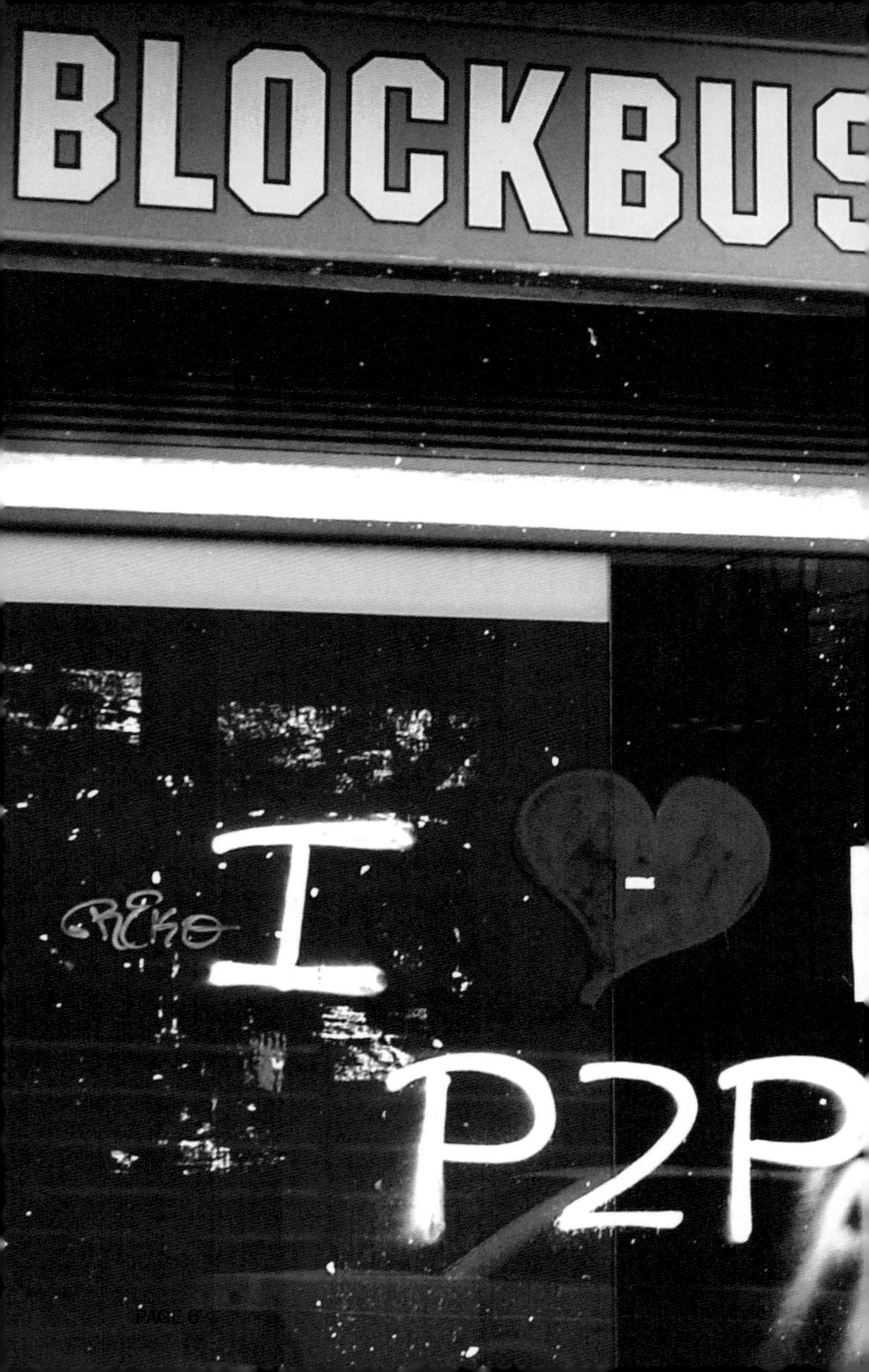
BLOCKBUS
I
P2P

WHAT HAPPENED HERE IS HAPPENING EVERYWHERE.

The list of companies — and industries — that have been disrupted by these changes is a long one. Companies like Blockbuster and Borders. Industries such as music, publishing, and retail. Here's what's happening:

DISRUPTIVE TECHNOLOGIES

DISRUPTIVE CHANGES

- Capabilities
- Expectations
- Perceptions
- Functionality
- Accessibility
- Habits

STUPID COMPANIES	SMART CUSTOMERS	SMART COMPANIES
Unable or unwilling to change, failing, marginalized, uncompetitive	Empowered, demanding, self-directed, and choosing to do business with smart companies	Intelligent, innovative, thriving, designed to do business with smart customers
NO FUTURE	**BRIGHT FUTURE**	

One:
Smart
Customers

DIGITAL INNOVATION IS LEAVING COMPANIES BEHIND

Today, customers can see, learn about, or purchase almost anything from almost anywhere.

In the midst of the Christmas season, Tri Tang spotted a Garmin GPS unit while visiting his local Best Buy store in Sunnyvale, California. He took out his Android phone and checked the price. The unit was $184.85 in the store, but $106.75 on Amazon, with no shipping or tax charges. Still standing in the store, he bought the GPS from Amazon.[1]

We hope he doesn't mind us saying so, but Tri is an early example of a new breed of customers. We call them smart customers.

Business executives get numb to the flood of buzzwords that proliferate these days, and as a result many tend to discount predictions. But the scope of intelligence now being handed to customers is unprecedented.

You can experience the results in a rapidly growing variety of fashions: see data overlays on a map or camera image, watch a video demonstration, or even have an explanation read to you.

EVERY DIGITAL DEVICE CREATES THE POTENTIAL TO SENSE WHAT'S HAPPENING – AND REMEMBER IT.

What you (and your customers) want, when you want it.

Buying a used car? Via CARFAX or AutoCheck, you can get its complete history, revealing whether it has been treated better or worse than the owner claims. Shopping for a gift, you can analyze whether the product recommended by the salesperson really is the best choice for your aunt, whether the store really does offer the lowest prices on that item, and whether a better-priced item is available within ten miles. Traveling at the last minute on business? Hotel Tonight can find you a great deal on a room that meets your personal preferences.

Why is this happening now?

Computers are so portable, powerful, and pervasive that they are our constant companions. For most of us, they are always connected. The iPhone opened the floodgates of innovation by independent developers who now have the hope of selling anything they can build, and a growing number of smartphones and tablets are pouring onto the market.

All of these factors combine to let people behave in a far smarter and better-informed manner. Yes, we know that lots of time is wasted watching dumb videos, making dumb videos, and texting your friends about dumb videos. But when it comes to money, to actual transactions, companies have to face a new reality.

"TO STAY AHEAD OF THE COMMODITIZATION STEAMROLLER SEEKING TO SQUEEZE MARGINS AND FLATTEN PROFITS, A COMPANY MUST ATTUNE ITSELF TO THE GREATEST SOURCE OF OFFERING INNOVATION EVER DEVISED: DIGITAL TECHNOLOGY."
— B. JOSEPH PINE II, CO-AUTHOR, *INFINITE POSSIBILITY: CREATING CUSTOMER VALUE ON THE DIGITAL FRONTIER*

It's the rise of smart customers.

We're not saying customers can leap tall buildings, but they can outwit your salesperson, easily spot misstatements by customer service reps, and have near instant access to the accumulated knowledge of human civilization. The trend is only just beginning, and you'll see it accelerate in the months ahead.

By the way, customers don't have to be on the go to have access to intelligence. Good old-fashioned laptops and desktops also provide access to increasingly powerful tools. Google's search refines your terms as you type them – the results shift as you make revisions – and it can find the information you need in mere seconds.

One of the key shifts is that you no longer have to be at your desk to have access to information. Smartphones and tablets now power data historically housed in mainframe computers whenever and wherever you want it.

CUSTOMERS START GAINING SUPERHERO POWERS

Any customer with a portable digital device (there will be many varieties) and the right combination of free or low-priced applications can now be something close to:

- **All-knowing,** having instant access not just to facts, figures, prices, and product specifications, but also billions of sensors around the world that help them better understand everything that happens in their lives;

- **Multilingual,** able to communicate in any language;

- **Omnipresent,** able to respond instantly as products and opportunities become available that match pre-set triggers they have instructed their applications to watch for;

- **Incredibly insightful,** spotting patterns in data and emerging trends because they have immense computing power at their fingertips and because they can immerse themselves in this data in dozens of different ways;

- **Ultra-aware,** using devices to augment what they see, hear, and smell so that they can deepen their experiences and better pursue their goals;

- **Supersensitive,** noticing sights, sounds, and changes that happen far away – on far larger (and smaller) scales than they could ever have noticed before, thanks to the sensors described above.

Smart customers are right here, right now.

We're not talking about sometime a decade out. Right now, smart customers can "see" traffic jams two miles ahead – and avoid them. They can "sniff out" delicious food being prepared 5.4 miles away – and reserve a table at that top-ranked restaurant in an instant. They can "hear" the falsehoods in the voice of a pushy, unethical salesperson and recognize the precise factual errors he has stated – and locate elsewhere exactly the price, features, and delivery they require.

You haven't seen anything yet.

At present, most customers are content to leave a trail of personal data behind them. They give Facebook permission to not only store but also broadcast vast amounts of data in their personal profiles.

They give online merchants permission to remember their credit card number, transactions, and Web browsing activity. They don't remove cookies from their browsers, making it possible for advertisers to track their movements online and target them with specific advertisements.

But what happens when customers take control of their data? This is inevitable, because there is a huge (Google/Amazon huge) opportunity for a new entity to be 100 percent on the side of customers, making it possible for them to share – and take back – all of the data related to their activities.

IT'S YOUR LIFE. ISN'T IT YOUR DATA?

Customers leave ever-larger digital footprints across markets, channels, and media.

In a world in which memory is everywhere, it is inevitable that human beings will resist having their lives reduced to a series of data points under the control of – and mismanaged by – others.

Smart customers are awakening to the fact that companies are using the data they generate for financial gain, and they wish to reclaim ownership. In other words, you should be able to access, manage, and earn money from the data that describes your life and activities and - if you choose - forbid others from using it.

> "We are not seats or eyeballs or end users or consumers. We are human beings, and our reach exceeds your grasp. Deal with it."

Chris Locke wrote these words for the 1999 book, *The Cluetrain Manifesto*, and Doc Searls – one of the book's co-authors – uses them to explain ProjectVRM, a research and development project of the Berkman Center for Internet & Society at Harvard University, which intends to spur the development of tools that help individuals take control of their data in the marketplace.

Doc believes that customer reach will only exceed vendor grasp when customers acquire tools for the job. Vendor Relationship Management (VRM) or Personal Identity Management (PIDM) give power to individuals who recognize their value as customers – and wish to better define the terms of their relationships with organizations – with the tools, software, and ability to do so.

Imagine selling a $100 item to a customer online, but being prohibited by both the customer and the law from storing any information about that transaction. Your firm will be flying in the dark, having to start each quarter from scratch, not remembering what you sold to whom last quarter.

A perfect storm is approaching.

The technology exists to make data portable. The profit incentive exists for venture capitalists to fund aggressive start-ups who see the immense potential of giving customers full control over their data. Most importantly, the majority of established companies don't use customer data to benefit their customers. It's all sell and no serve.

When this storm hits, numerous companies will be disintermediated. Entire industries will be transformed. Some companies will go from having superficial relationships with their customers to having no relationships at all. For them, "loyalty" will be a thing of the past.

Since it is easier to establish a culture from scratch than reinvent the culture of a large organization, new competitors will surface that possess truly customer-focused cultures. These cultures will invent new services that no inward facing, self-absorbed, siloed enterprise could imagine.

Since this is a book for business executives, customer experience professionals, and entrepreneurs, let's get right to the bottom line...

COMPANIES CAN'T BE COMPETITIVE IF THEY CAN'T STAY AHEAD OF THEIR CUSTOMERS

Smart customers can spot a lie. They won't tolerate wasted time. For at least the next few years, as companies struggle to get as smart as the customers they serve, smart customers will have better access to information than many of your employees.

They also will have more choices, more flexibility, and more negotiating power.

If you run a successful and established business, this might be a terrifying proposition.

It can put your margins under pressure. This is even happening at Apple, which is rumored to have 40 percent profit margins on its Mac line, but just 25 percent margins on iPads.[3] Just before the March 2012 launch of the new iPad, the *Washington Post* reported that Apple's total sales of iPads had reached 55 million.[4] But Apple has an ace in the hole.

Each iPad creates a revenue stream after it is sold because customers download dozens of apps. Some are free, but an increasing percentage of these provide Apple with incremental revenue.

"The iPad is not just a product that Apple makes and throws out there in the market. It's a platform," according to Michael Cusumano, Professor of Management and Engineering Systems at the Massachusetts Institute of Technology Sloan School of Management.

> **"AN INNOVATION IS ONE OF THOSE THINGS THAT SOCIETY LOOKS AT AND SAYS, IF WE MAKE THIS PART OF THE WAY WE LIVE AND WORK, IT WILL CHANGE THE WAY WE LIVE AND WORK."**
> — DEAN KAMEN, INVENTOR AND SERIAL ENTREPRENEUR

It can put loyalty under pressure. Already the rise of smart customers is undercutting loyalty: people download price comparison apps to find the lowest price, which implies constant switching and disloyalty. It threatens to dissolve – perhaps in months – the advantages your business may have gained by investing millions in bricks and mortar. Most importantly, it can turn size and scale into disadvantages.

Each day, firms such as Groupon and LivingSocial blast out emails that offer 50 percent off of retail items, restaurants, and personal services. Google has been testing a similar service called Google Offers. Countless other services ask consumers to tell them the brands and products they prefer, and then send customized offers. All of these are teaching customers to expect and respond to personalized deals.

It's easier for customers to get smarter than for companies.

To get smarter, a customer merely signs up for such a service, or downloads an app. As we'll discuss later, large businesses are dependent on enterprise software, complex processes, and inflexible organizational structures — all of which are very slow and expensive to change.

Pretty much everything we have mentioned so far has already happened. The 2010 holiday season was the first in which customers in large numbers stood in retail stores, scanned product barcodes into their phones, and ordered that same item online because they could save $10, $20, or $100.

DISRUPTIVE FORCES + SMART CUSTOMERS MEANS THAT COMPANIES MUST SHIFT THEIR STRATEGIES.

tra

link
everything

get more
granular

IN

make
loyalty
convenient

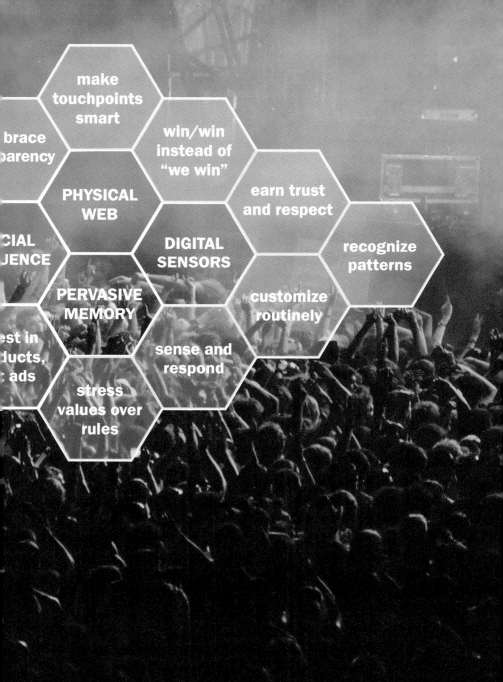

make
touchpoints
smart

brace
parency

win/win
instead of
"we win"

PHYSICAL
WEB

earn trust
and respect

CIAL
UENCE

DIGITAL
SENSORS

recognize
patterns

PERVASIVE
MEMORY

customize
routinely

est in
ucts,
ads

sense and
respond

stress
values over
rules

**The rise of smart customers has started,
but this trend is in its infancy.**

The velocity of change and expansion this represents is staggering. The disruptive forces being unleashed now are changing customer experience forever.

As brand loyalty continues to erode, staying ahead of these changing customer expectations means that everywhere a company interacts with or "touches" a customer, those interactions need to be smarter, faster, and better.

Smarter interactions turn complaints into upsells, reveal customer needs, drive loyalty, create new revenue streams, and power innovation.

Yet many companies don't fully understand these forces, much less the changes that will be wrought on their industries. They continue to treat customers the same as ever, with little understanding or concern for the growing discontent their ever-empowered customer base is feeling.

Today, even the youngest, most modest consumer has broadband Internet access at home, and many carry powerful, interconnected mobile devices everywhere they go. This gives them access to products, services, and information from anywhere, at anytime – on their terms and their schedule.

"FOR TOO LONG WE HAVE BEEN LEADING OUR COMPANIES AND OPERATING OUR BUSINESSES BASED ON 19TH AND 20TH CENTURY APPROACHES THAT DON'T RESONATE IN THIS NEW WORLD."
— DOV SEIDMAN, AUTHOR OF
HOW: WHY HOW WE DO ANYTHING MEANS EVERYTHING

Leveraging these devices from home, school, and work, today's customers quickly access myriad databases and technological tools from dozens of different sources. As a result, the average customer (whether business or consumer) often knows more about pricing, availability, and market demand than the companies from which they buy.

This is increasingly true around the globe.

Your customers are getting less patient – and your younger customers never had much patience to begin with.

Then there are the adults who have grown up with the Web and text messaging. Anyone 20 or younger has never known a world without the Web. The oldest of this generation are now adults, soon to graduate from college and start households of their own. They are already potent consumers, buying music, games, clothing, and other items in large numbers.

To generalize just a little, these people have seldom experienced the maddening, inexplicable customer service disappointments most grownups have come to accept. Why? Because often their parents took care of these "money" issues. So now as they enter the world as adults, they expect everything to be connected, to be digital, and to be instant.

Importantly, the economic clout they represent is increasing.

But you know most of this already. The tough part is thinking through the implications for your business, for the types of new products and services you can offer, and for your industry as a whole.

Yes, this is being driven by smartphones.

There's little doubt that these forces are being driven in large part by the adoption of smartphones. There are now 1.2 billion active mobile broadband subscriptions in the world, representing 17 percent of the world population.[5]

In the United States, mobile users are using their phones to shop and buy from wherever they are. As an example, 60 percent of mobile buyers do so from home,[6] and 70 percent of iPhone owners use apps while shopping in-store.[7] Add this to the fact that the majority of shoppers believe that smartphones make shopping more enjoyable, and you see why we say that customers increasingly expect 24/7 attention from smart companies.

This isn't just a North American trend; this is happening everywhere, all at once.

According to a recent Nielsen report, Chinese youth lead in mobile Internet usage; nearly three-quarters of those aged 15 to 24 have used the mobile Internet in the past 30 days. The next highest levels of usage were in the United States at nearly 50 percent and Russia at nearly 40 percent.[8]

While the forces we describe in this book go far beyond any single telecommunications device, the rapid adoption of smartphones and tablets certainly give customers instant and ever-present access to intelligence.

When half the people with mobile phones have smartphones,[9] it's safe to say that at least half your customers today are far smarter than your customers used to be.

But it's not just smartphones: the rise of machines, and other connected devices.

As ubiquitous as mobile phones may be, they're simply the leading device in an always-on, fully connected, data-hungry world. As projected by Cisco in its "Global Mobile Data Traffic Forecast Update, 2010-2015," global mobile data traffic will increase 26-fold between 2010 and 2015.[10]

While smartphones, laptops, and netbooks continue to generate a disproportionate amount of traffic, new categories of devices will account for a significant portion by 2015.

These include tablets, gaming consoles, sensors, eReaders, televisions, and even our cars, as well as Machine-to-Machine (M2M) devices that include wireless and wired sensors or meters that capture and relay information and data about events like temperature, inventory levels, and more.

There are trillions of digital sensors and devices out there today, with millions more being deployed every month.

Connected customers and the Internet of Things.

We're quickly moving towards the Internet of Things (IOT), when most objects in the world can be identified, and physical objects will seamlessly integrate into the global information network.

In this world, people and services will interact with these devices over the Internet, queries will be answered automatically and information will be distributed (and action taken) based on pre-determined rules, requirements, and conditions.

Smart touchpoints, products, services, and objects will work together so businesses almost always know when, where, and what people buy and consume, and customers will almost always know where to find what they need, exactly when they need it.

As these trends – which until recently could be labeled science fiction – continue to become mainstream, customers can tap into, organize, and leverage the incredible insights collected by social networks, the data that accumulates through pervasive memory, and the knowledge and insight being gathered by digital sensors...and get to it anytime, from almost anywhere.

This means that wherever your customers are, it's not simply that they *can* access the products, services, or information in which they are interested. They actively *are* accessing it – from your company, your competitors, and each other.

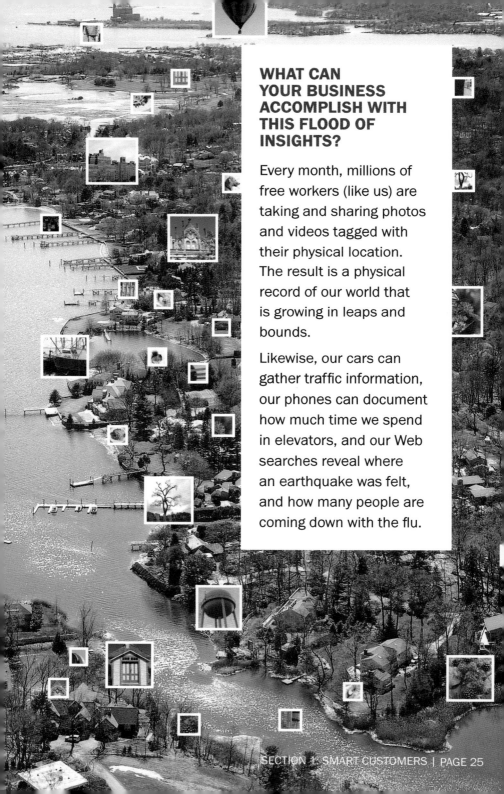

WHAT CAN YOUR BUSINESS ACCOMPLISH WITH THIS FLOOD OF INSIGHTS?

Every month, millions of free workers (like us) are taking and sharing photos and videos tagged with their physical location. The result is a physical record of our world that is growing in leaps and bounds.

Likewise, our cars can gather traffic information, our phones can document how much time we spend in elevators, and our Web searches reveal where an earthquake was felt, and how many people are coming down with the flu.

SMART CUSTOMERS EXPECT SMART CUSTOMER EXPERIENCES

Smart customers want to talk to, access, interact with, and ask questions of your company. Right now. From wherever they may be.

We live in a world in which whether you are out in the woods, at a client's business, or in your living room, you can connect information and processing power with people and devices that need it right here and right now.

This is a giant departure for everything that has come before in business, life, and the world. Today, unless there's something wrong with our phones or computer, we are almost never without access to guidance, to others, to ideas, and to possibilities.

None of this is to suggest that data silos are a thing of the past, or that every company has made their products, services or data available remotely 24/7. To the contrary, most companies still bury vast quantities of data where it is inaccessible and often unusable.

How smart are your employees?

Ironically, smart customers have the ability to access information in this "anytime, anywhere" manner. But when these individuals are acting as employees, the story often changes.

A Motorola Solutions annual holiday shopping survey revealed that 55 percent of surveyed retailers cite shoppers as better connected to information than store associates.[11]

"Retailers have put their associates at a significant disadvantage to connected consumers," said Frank Riso, Senior Director of Retail Solutions for Motorola Solutions. "With 87 percent of surveyed retail associates noting that shoppers can easily find a better deal,[12] offering the best customer experience is more important than ever. Retailers need to arm their mobile associates with access to real-time information to level the shopping playing field."

This doesn't mean your firm will act smart, only that it should.

Some companies have the technology, willpower, and funding to provide remote access to vital data. These companies are using data to drive innovation.

They are successfully using remote access to data and services to revolutionize their industries, and this trend is accelerating. Even so, there are many firms that are unwilling or slow to react.

For every technology-enabled UPS or FedEx driver, there are dozens if not hundreds of employees at other firms who are forced to sit at desks and use internal systems that are slow, unreliable, and inaccurate – or wander the aisles of their stores, calling for price checks and inventory availability over the PA system.

CASE STUDY, CIRCA 2015

"Mommy, why won't the TV answer me?"

Julia stood in front of the television set, wailing. Her mom rushed down the basement stairs to see what was troubling the little girl. "What's wrong, baby?"

Her daughter gave her a look of confusion and hurt. "She won't answer me, Mommy. Why won't she answer me?"

Katie smiled. Julia was standing in front of their old TV, which Bill last night decided to pull out of the garage and set up in front of the treadmill.

"She won't play Sesame Street! She won't turn up the music!"

Katie crouched and put her arms around the little girl. "This TV is old, Julia. It doesn't talk. It doesn't listen."

Julia rubbed her eyes. "Everything talks, Mommy. Toaster talks. Fridge talks. Garage talks. Why won't TV talk?"

"No, honey, just a few years ago nothing but people talked. None of the things around our house used to talk. So anything that's older than you probably can't talk."

Julia tilted her head. "But that's stupid, Mommy. How do things know what you want if they can't talk and they can't hear?"

Katie smiled. "We used to have to push buttons, twist knobs and type on keyboards. Everything had controls you touched with your hands."

"Yuck," said Julia with a grimace. "Dirty."

"Maybe a little bit, yes." It certainly was easier to keep appliances and electronics clean, now that you barely touched them.

Julia looked back at the TV. "Old TV is stupid. Old toasters are stupid, too. Everything old is stupid."

Katie looked her daughter in the eye. "I'm sort of old. Am I stupid?"

Julia shook her head aggressively. "No, Mommy. You can talk. You listen to me. You're not stupid. Only things that don't listen are stupid."

Wow, thought Katie, Julia's generation will only know intelligent devices. Her daughter still had trouble holding a crayon properly, but she was creating stories just by talking to the bulletin board next to her bed. At night, Julia would chat happily with "Sarah," and Sarah would record every word the little girl said – unless Julia told her to "forget that last part."

Katie had to admit it was an unsettling change when the first few companies made the transition from horrific voicemail systems to Talking Company. Now you could just call Best Buy and a gentle female voice knew every detail about every product; she even remembered your previous call.

"Mommy," said Julia, trying to get her Mom to focus on what is really important. "Please make the stupid TV play Sesame Street."

We used to watch TV when TV networks told us the show was on, or to do our banking between 9 a.m. and 3 p.m., when banks preferred to do business. No more.

One of our kids recently walked into a room where his family members were watching a television show as it was being initially aired. In other words, we couldn't fast forward through the commercials.

"What, are you stupid?" he asked bluntly. "Why would you do that?" He was genuinely stumped.

The accelerometer is one of many sensors routinely included in smartphones, revealing how the phone – and you – are moving through and interacting with the physical world. Soon, altimeters, heart-rate monitors, and environmental sensors will join a rapidly growing list, allowing your phone to sense you, and the world around you.

> **"CHANGE IS THE LAW OF LIFE. AND THOSE WHO LOOK ONLY TO THE PAST OR PRESENT ARE CERTAIN TO MISS THE FUTURE."**
> — PRESIDENT JOHN F. KENNEDY

Why "sorry, we're closed" means you may be closed forever.

There are still many businesses where customer service and support is provided only during certain hours: if you call after, say, 7 p.m. Pacific Time, technical support is closed. Seriously? Does the firm really expect that none of their products are installed or used after 7 p.m.?

These sort of time-based restrictions are going to disappear for companies that successfully embrace the changed notion of customer service and customer experience.

Not because it suddenly becomes profitable to stay open 24/7. But because when you compete with firms like Zappos, which operates their warehouse 24/7 even though it's not the most efficient way to do so, the notion of being "closed" will become suicidal from a competitive perspective.

Competitors like these recognize that the value of delighting customers who order after midnight with a shipment that shows up on their doorsteps literally hours after being ordered can't be measured by "maximized picking efficiency."

They're measuring the value of providing "a wow experience, which (their) customers remember for a very long time and tell their friends and family about."[13]

These trends and forces have combined to alter customer expectations.

Customers expect to do anything they want, from anywhere and at any time. Why? Because they can – and they already do.

In some industries, this tremendously changes the expectations for what comprises good customer service.

We are living in a world in which customers can shift time and space at will to meet their needs. Resisting these trends is a dangerous thing for a company to do.

This doesn't just mean that more people are going to be working the night shift. It also means that companies will leverage technology to diagnose problems, train customers, upsell services, and gather feedback.

The question that we're helping your company answer is this: How can you leverage these trends to not only catch up to, but stay ahead of, your competition and your customers?

KEY TAKEAWAYS:

- Digital devices will increasingly give individuals "super" powers to sense, remember, analyze, understand, and share insights from the world around them.

- Companies must use customer information to benefit the customer.

- Disruptive forces will require massive changes in your company's strategy.

- Your company must be able to act smarter than its customers, or it will cease to exist.

Two:
Intelligence is Everywhere

BEYOND 1to1 TO 1toEVERYTHING

If you think our world has been overrun by technology, think again. It's hard to imagine what is now possible, yet still untapped.

For the next few days, try this: wherever you go, imagine everything being collected to the Web. Imagine that by clicking, touching or perhaps just looking at an object, you could know everything about it.

While nearly everyone you know has a smartphone, most objects and living creatures have yet to be connected to the larger Web.

1toEverything is going to change this. It's a way of thinking about how any individual can interact with the world around him, and imagining what companies will have to do to keep up with customers in this new world.

Years ago, ambitious marketers looked at their customers and saw a 1to1 future.

Today, innovators look through the eyes of their customers and they see a 1toEverything future.

1 is the customer. Everything is every person, creature, element, and piece of information on the planet.

(Of course, the customer is just a person. She doesn't think: "I am a customer." She may have no active connection with any company. We use the word "customer" because our ultimate objective is to help companies win, keep, and grow their number of customers.)

Bruce was one of the original partners of the 1to1 marketing consultancy, Peppers and Rogers Group. Don Peppers and Martha Rogers popularized the idea that firms ought to treat different customers differently, a strategy they termed 1to1 marketing.

They built their strategy around a framework they called IDIC, which stands for:

1. Identify   **3. Interact**

2. Differentiate   **4. Customize**

The 1to1 mantra basically goes: *Identify* customers individually; *differentiate* your treatment of customers based on their needs and value; *interact* individually with customers; then *customize* products and services for each profitable customer.

This framework has proven its value over nearly two decades, across numerous industries, and through widely changing economic conditions.

It can take awhile to internalize IDIC: The concept is not difficult, but the applications are nearly unlimited, and many only become apparent the more you use it.

You can turn IDIC around and use it to predict how customers are likely to leverage the interactive technologies that are now part of our lives.

IDENTIFY ANYTHING, ANYWHERE, ANYTIME

For the purposes of this book, we're going to focus on the first three steps: Identify, Differentiate, and Interact.

This is because the first three steps take place at the present moment while the fourth, Customize, generally refers to the opportunity for a company to learn from the interaction and – based on this learning – customize treatment of customers in subsequent interactions.

That's more of a general principle, while the first three require some explanation to make clear.

1to1 is about looking at individual customers through the company's eyes.

What does IDIC look like through a customer's eyes?

An even more powerful use of Don and Martha's framework might be to look at innovation from the customer's perspective. How do customers feel? What are they looking for? Flipping this perspective means companies should be more concerned with what customers want than with how they interact with them.

Using the three capabilities described above, you can redesign nearly any customer experience. Even better, you can start to figure out how to deliver that experience.

What does IDIC look like through a customer's eyes? Simply turn the page to see...

1toEVERYTHING

Identify anything by ...	Differentiate it by ...	Interact with the results ...

A Person:
- Opinions
- Skills
- Needs
- Wants
- Emotions
- Health
- Characteristics

An Object, Place or Entity:
- Name
- Locations
- Features
- Composition
- Uses
- Cost
- Value

An Event:
- Transaction
- Interaction
- Gathering

- Personal preferences
- Business specifications
- Price
- Quality
- Components
- Uses
- Trends
- Proximity
- Reliability
- Compatibility
- Reviews/opinions
- Delivery
- Trust
- Risk
- Pleasure
- Ease of use
- Effectiveness

Learn and Explore:
- Browse/surf
- Read
- Watch
- Listen
- Discuss
- Simulate
- Analyze
- Demo

Purchase:
- Product
- Service
- Support

Immerse:
- Game
- Education
- Entertainment
- Communication
- Community

The blank box at the top of each column allows you to pick an example from each column that is relevant to your customers and your business. The examples in each column are just that; they are not intended to be inclusive of the nearly infinite possibilities.

A FRAMEWORK FOR INFINITE OPPORTUNITY AND INNOVATION

Let's use a simple example to demonstrate the degree to which everywhere you look, these three capabilities create opportunities.

Look out your window. Imagine you are home and you see a rhododendron, some bamboo, and some lavender plants. Your phone, backed by pattern recognition software, is theoretically capable of:

- Identifying each plant;

- Differentiating each based on your current needs and interests (which ones need mulch to survive the winter?);

- Interacting with the results in an immersive experiential manner, for example, showing you how big a three-year-old lavender plant should be compared to yours, or having a video pop up to demonstrate the right way to apply fertilizer in the late fall.

Identify almost anything.

Until now, this sort of identification has been pretty narrow: customers are increasingly used to checking prices and searching for books, movies, or music with their devices.

But it's possible to identify almost anything. Instead of searching for a 2012 Toyota Corolla, a customer can search for *his* Toyota Corolla...in a big parking lot, perhaps.

Instead of relying on his fallible memory, a customer can search for the perfect picnic spot he found at the crest of the hill while hiking in Wyoming last year (and that he tagged virtually).

In such a way, his phone becomes a virtual tour guide, leading him back to the exact spot and providing an easy way to send friends to the very same place. This also creates options for virtual tour guides around the world.

Differentiate it from myriad options.

Once a customer has identified one or maybe even one hundred possibilities, the next step is to differentiate it from other options. With each passing year, humanity is generating, storing, and organizing more information – all of which can be used to help in this process.

Identify (exactly) what you want.

Your customer – or patient – may not simply be seeking a capable physician, but specifically a Board-certified internist who has a holistic mindset and also embraces alternative therapies and understands the unique needs of people who have recently spent extended periods of time in developing tropical countries.

Answering this need requires more than mere access to social network recommendations; it also requires the active cooperation of such physicians.

IDENTIFY	DIFFERENTIATE	INTERACT
Customer "tags" his grocery store as a location at which he can receive reminders from himself	Customer sees ad for bean dip on TV, and sends a note to himself	Three days later, as he enters store, customer receives a reminder to pick up bean dip
Golf balls are sold with personal sensors inside	Sensors track spin, flight paths and ultimate location of ball	On smartphone, golfer sees degree of hook/ slice on each shot and adjusts on next round
Each item in a clothing store has a smart tag attached to it	Shopper scans a tag, then scans other items to see if their color/style match the initial choice	Customer more quickly acquires items that coordinate perfectly
Automated voice recognition system answers customer phone calls and listens (no button-pushing necessary)	System can answer questions, trigger response by computer or device (e.g. cable box), or get customer to the right person	Customer gets a prompt and correct answer. The experience is simple and satisfying
Customer points phone camera at an item	App shows customer how to install and use the product	Customer never has to touch a manual or call customer service

These are just examples. We suggest you use these three steps to look at different customer segments you serve. How might a customer within each segment identify, differentiate, and interact with elements in the world around them? How could your business make these interactions richer?

INNOVATORS LOOK THROUGH THE EYES OF THEIR CUSTOMERS

The benefits for customers are endless.

As illustrated on the previous page, benefits to customers might mean making "just the right purchase," getting a vexing technical issue resolved, or having a picture painted right before their eyes.

It could mean having a highly trained professional showing up in person, or virtually via a video or interactive demo. The results might be displayed on a smart phone or on a touchscreen as large as a wall.

It takes Big Data to unlock this innovation. Good thing. Big Data is getting bigger by the second.

Virtually all firms of scale gather terabytes of data on their operations and their customers. Yet according to Forrester Research, Inc., most effectively utilize less than five percent of available data.[1] Why so little? Because the rest has been too costly with which to deal.

The concept of Big Data means that firms can cost effectively analyze the remaining 95 percent of this data, driving new insights and competitive advantages for those who do so.

Jim Baum, CEO of Netezza, the data warehouse appliance firm IBM acquired in 2010 for $1.7 billion,[2] says, "We have customers who are looking to optimize the real estate on the Internet, or their analyses of clinical healthcare trials, or smartgrids, or truck routes.

The common thread across all of those is the concept of Big Data as the underlying enabler because in some industries we're approaching a level of technical sophistication where they can have something approaching ubiquitous data collection from all this sensing detection at the point of use – it's just exploding."

Baum was talking to *InformationWeek*'s Bob Evans, who observes, "For some companies, that'll just mean ever-larger storage purchases to hold all that new data, but aggressive and forward-looking companies will look at those data as prized raw materials that, with the right analytical tools, can be mined, refined, and turned into cash."

Evans wrote that the eventual payback of IBM's investment in Netezza is the ability to deliver "business analytics to the masses." In other words, IBM – which has been aggressively pushing its Smarter Planet theme – plans to become a major enabler of smarter customers, too.

Looking at opportunities through 1toEverything can help firms anticipate where analytics for the masses will go.

What do customers want to know? What services will entrance them? Where are the best opportunities for innovation? What services could competitors bring to our industry, and should we do it first? Look through the lens of 1toEverything and see.

WHAT YOUR CUSTOMERS COULD DO WITH A PAIR OF SMART GLASSES

Tint or no tint?

First, let's assume that, as some lenses do already, your new glasses can shift from sunglasses to clear glasses – with one important difference. When they darken, they can function as virtual displays, showing you information overlays of any type.

Embedded micro cameras solve vision challenges.

Your glasses will include at least two, and probably more, cameras. The cameras will provide your glasses with the ability to zoom into anything you see, and display the results right in your glasses. In other words, instead of simply seeing the world directly, each lens is also a display. In one fell swoop, this could help vision problems from minor near-sightedness to macular degeneration.

Record your entire life, or just a few joyous moments.

Your eyeglass cameras have the capability to record every moment of your waking life from critical business meetings to special moments with your family – or, more practically, where you last put your keys, or wallet.

Using facial recognition and pattern recognition software, you can search for specific people, places, events, and content. To prevent certain moments from ever being erased, you can speak to your glasses, saying something like, "Glasses: protect the past five minutes."

Night vision, heat sensing, or x-ray?

Data processing will enable some amazing enhancements to your video feeds. Driving on a dark country road at night, you'll be able to enable night vision or even heat sensing; the latter can help you avoid hitting deer or other animals that cluster by the side of a road and sometimes dart into it.

You might even have x-ray vision that enables you to see through, well, clothes (strictly for security purposes, of course).

Sensors focus your attention.

Just as your phone does now, your glasses will include a number of sensors that identify which direction you are facing, and whether your head is tilted, moving, or not.

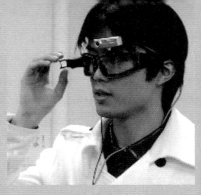

Researchers at the University of Tokyo have developed "video goggles." Through high-speed image recognition, they analyze, name, and file everything the wearer looks at, storing data in an easily searchable database.

The GPS capabilities of your phone already provide a way to identify where you are, but attaching sensors to your head can provide a much richer set of data about what you are doing — and why. For example, such sensors might reveal that you seldom look people in the eye, or that you fail to do so when you are not certain of what you are saying.

They could demonstrate that you lift your head when playing tennis, spend too much time looking at the dashboard when you are driving, or that the reason your back always hurts is because you generally tilt your head nine degrees to the left.

No more writing. No more paper.

Now that you can record and replay everything you see and hear, there will be no need for students to take notes or business people to write meeting memos. People will simply share feeds from their glasses, or automatically transcribe text summaries of certain meetings and events.

Social matters become clear.

Can't remember what your boss's wife looks like, or her name? No problem; your glasses remember, and can literally whisper her name into your ear.

If you so choose, your "social adviser" can remind you about the birthdays, job titles, and kids of the people to whom you are speaking. The advisor will even be able to recall past interactions, and whisper key facts back to you.

Time for a reality check.

Are we two years or ten away from such innovations becoming commercially available? We don't know for sure, but the truth is, nearly every capability we have mentioned is already available in one form or another.

From facial recognition to automatic digital video capture of every waking hour of a person's life, these technologies are already here. The next step is making them small, cheap, and easy enough to use that millions embrace these capabilities.

Our point is not to sell glasses. It's to demonstrate that nearly everything about the way we live and work is about to change. We will become (even more) dependent on tiny tools that make our lives easier. This wave will help us differentiate individual people, objects, and events from everything else in the world.

Available today for around $400, Zeal Optics' sensor-laden iON ski goggles boast HD video and camera, and a GPS-linked heads-up display.[3] Real-time speed, altitude, time and temp, plus a "memory" of every twist and turn may render some ski stories obsolete. ("Dude, what do you mean that was only a 5-foot drop? No way!")

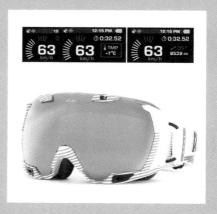

TECHNOLOGY IS MAGIC YOUR CUSTOMERS NEED TO TRUST

Your customers want sophisticated technologies to remove – not add – complexity from their lives.

Back in the mid 1990s, Bruce worked on the IBM account at Ogilvy & Mather. This was when the agency and its client defined IBM's brand as representing technology that's "magic you can trust." This is what most customers want today, and not just from IBM.

Like a magician seeking novel ways to create new tricks, your company needs to seek new ways to mix and match new technologies to provide magical customer experiences in a manner that generates sustainable profits.

Today, customers want products so easy and intuitive to use that they require neither manuals nor late night calls to tech support, much less the need to change the ways they think, work or interact with technology already.

It's not just magic you can trust, it's magic your customers don't even think about.

There's a video circulating online of a little toddler being handed a new iPad by her parents, and the two year old girl instantly realizes she can just touch the screen. She clicks on a drawing program, and just as quickly realizes she can draw with her hands.

This is a quality customer experience: seamless, enjoyable, and intuitive. It's the future, and it's already here.

NO MANUALS.
NO KEYBOARDS.
NO LIMITS.

No, not all customers are kids. Or retail consumers.

The world is also filled with business customers buying from other companies. Of course, they are also human, and many currently endure clumsy, non-intuitive interfaces. They deal with vendors whose staff never seem to talk to each other, or who actively contradict each other.

They can't find answers because databases aren't connected, or because their vendor's divisions don't cooperate with each other.

Today's business buyers are increasingly bringing their experiences and expectations as consumers to their roles as corporate decision makers. This is data we've seen proven out – to the almost universal consternation of our B2B clients – many times in the last three to four years.

These customers are changing their expectations too. They are using all the cool new devices we've been describing. They know what is possible. And when they ask questions and request new services, the stakes are even higher.

But we're getting ahead of ourselves. Before we take you through a brutally honest look at the state of most established firms – many of whom have already invested millions of dollars in customer-focused initiatives – let's look in depth through the disruptive forces changing customer experience.

KEY TAKEAWAYS:

- Individuals will use digital devices to identify and differentiate any one thing in the universe from everything else.

- Understanding how individuals (and everything else) differ from each other will help your company develop profitable new services.

- Everything from your garden to your glasses is going to get smart, and smart objects will create new business models.

- The more powerful a product is, the more intuitive it should be to use.

Three:
A Perfect Storm of Disruptive Innovation

THE FOUR DISRUPTIVE FORCES

**Disruptive innovation is making customers smarter.
It can make companies smarter, too.**

As the word "disruptive" suggests, this change is not happening in a steady and predictable way, but rather in a manner that most threatens established organizations, which are slower to change. The main question is pretty simple: Can your firm anticipate the impacts of these forces so that it gets smarter faster than competitors and customers?

These forces are not operating in isolation...the opposite is true: They are building on each other. This creates countless opportunities – but also dramatically raises the bar for delivering "ideal" (much less truly differentiated) customer experiences:

- Social Influence means that the opinions and experiences of countless other people come between your firm and its customers.

- Pervasive Memory makes it inevitable that companies will begin to profitably leverage the data generated by the trillions of interactions and transactions made through digital devices.

- Digital Sensors expand exponentially the scope of actions, events, and behaviors firms can sense...and to which they can respond.

- The rise of the Physical Web has begun. Today, we are linking objects and locations in the real world like we do on the Web.

These forces will require every business to rethink, and in many cases reinvent, their business models. They are not unpredictable, but potent and unavoidable.

"What level of customer experience must we provide, and how will we do it?" becomes a life or death question for senior executives, and the time to answer it is now.

Let's take a deeper look at each disruptive force, and then see how they are working together to make customers smarter, more demanding, and much tougher for most companies to serve.

THESE FORCES WILL CHANGE ENTIRE INDUSTRIES. IN FACT, THEY ARE PROBABLY CHANGING YOUR INDUSTRY RIGHT NOW.

THE PERFECT STORM OF DISRUPTIVE FORCES

Business Impact ↑

Business Value →

- Track Everything / Digital Sensors
- Remember Everything / Pervasive Memory
- Share Everything / Social Influence
- Do So Everywhere / Physical Web

DISRUPTIVE FORCE NUMBER ONE: SOCIAL INFLUENCE

Social Influence is the impact that social networks have on relationships between customers and companies.

It used to be that when a company engaged with a customer, few other parties were involved. Today, that's not the case.

Social networks create an environment in which customers are talking to other people, learning from other people, asking questions of other people...while they are also interacting with the company. Talk about a crowded relationship.

Of course, it could be worse than this. Social Influence has the potential to completely remove some companies from the equation. Even Google finds itself threatened by Facebook's ability to help its members find content online (that's one important goal of Facebook's "Like" buttons).

What does this mean to the leaders of a company? Others will challenge your claims. They will review and analyze the quality of your products, the degree to which your firm is trustworthy, and the degree to which you perform as promised. All of these will be tested, examined, discussed, and shared by other people even as the customer sits in front of you.

One of us was recently sitting with a friend in an office furniture store, testing chairs and talking to the sales rep. At the same time, we were using our smartphones to look at reviews of these chairs.

As the sales rep would tell us about a chair, we'd find a new review online. The opinions we were discovering became part of the conversation; we would see a review, mention an observation to the sales rep, and he would react to it. As a result, we were much better educated than we would have been in the past.

By the way, we also discovered that the chair we really liked – the one the rep said would take four weeks for delivery – was available online in three days. We left without buying the chair.

From the other side of this equation, the sales rep had to deal with the opinions of many people – none of whom were physically present in his store – as well as an invisible (to the rep) competitor.

Social Influence creates enormous issues for companies.

A recent survey sponsored by Cisco indicated that 63 percent of shoppers in the United States and the United Kingdom use technology to find the lowest price, while 47 percent use it to save time.[1]

Truth is, we haven't seen anything yet. Innovators around the world are hard at work trying to shift the balance of power away from companies and towards customers, using technology to empower individuals.

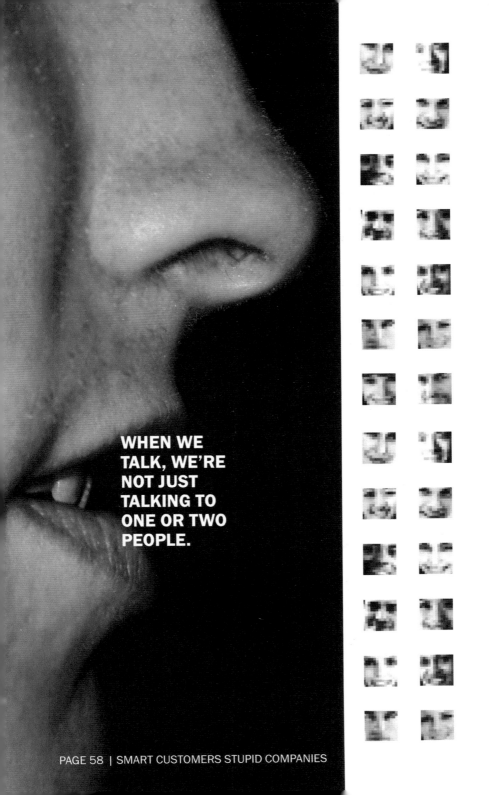

WHEN WE
TALK, WE'RE
NOT JUST
TALKING TO
ONE OR TWO
PEOPLE.

Due to the explosive growth of Facebook – it now has more than 845 million active members,[2] and more than 425 million access the site via mobile devices[3] – people tend to think of social networks as consisting mainly of that site, LinkedIn, Twitter, MySpace, Friendster, and a few dozen others.

Different countries have different social networks as well, though the boundaries are anything but clear, transcending social class, culture, geography, and other traditional demarcations to create entirely new centers of influence. Bebo in the UK, Renren and Pengyou in China, Badoo in Russia and Brazil, and invitation-only Tuenti in Spain.

Of course, the social media landscape will keep changing.

The constant will be the presence of other people and other opinions inserting their influence into what used to be a relatively closed relationship between a company and its customers.

Some people won't order from a website that lacks customer reviews. Others won't order from a firm unless that firm has credible customer feedback prominently displayed. By "credible," we mean that the firm transparently displays the good, the bad, and the ugly feedback.

Social Influence shifts the balance of power between companies and customers. It forces companies to be more open and honest, even when they would prefer not to be.

We are confronting a fundamental shift in the ways that companies interact with – and serve – their customers.

At many firms, their "social media strategy" involves creating a Facebook page, monitoring social sites for mentions of the company or its products, and generally extending its existing business model into the social media world.

But this approach stops short of confronting the real issues. If you could physically see the thousands of social influencers crowding the space between your sales team and your customers – if they were physically present in your store or office – you would no longer accept the misguided notion that a few extra posts online would solve your problems.

The reason so many companies are vulnerable is because the state of relationships between companies and customers is so poor. Products and services tend to be impersonal. Responsiveness tends to be uneven at best, or miserable at worst.

It is reasonable to assert that frustration, annoyance, and anger have been building among customers for decades. They are tired of being treated as numbers, of being misled or even lied to, and of being considered targets instead of living, breathing human beings.

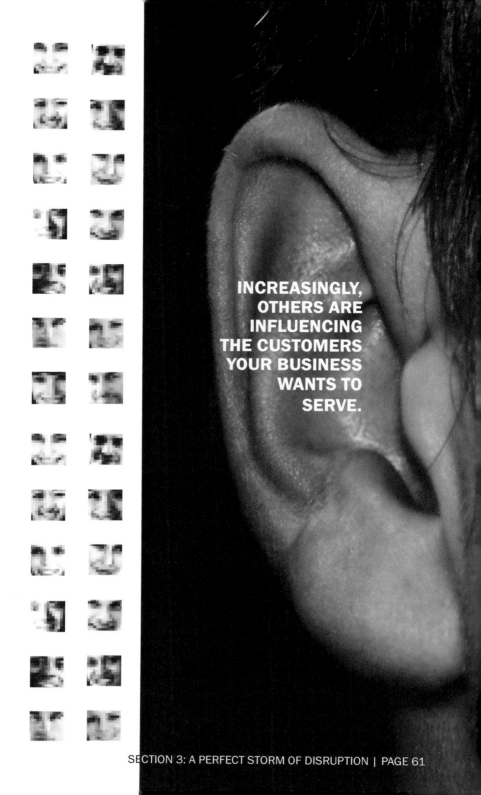

INCREASINGLY, OTHERS ARE INFLUENCING THE CUSTOMERS YOUR BUSINESS WANTS TO SERVE.

SOCIAL INFLUENCE: A CASE STUDY

Social Influence is sort of like democracy coming to a country that has only known a dictatorship. The current leadership thinks: It's an unmitigated disaster. The people think: Eureka, we are free at last!

This is precisely what happened across the Arab world in 2011, as Social Influence brought people together driving a wave of demonstrations and protests in over a dozen countries.

In Egypt, a 30-year-old Google executive named Wael Ghonim helped set up a Facebook page that was instrumental in sparking a chain of protests that toppled the country's leader.[4]

If Social Influence can change a country, it can certainly change the way customers do business with – or abandon – your company. As the *National* (the Abu Dhabi Media company's English-language publication) wrote:

> "The recent protests in Tunisia and Egypt have, more than ever before, successfully utilized social media like Twitter, Facebook and YouTube in the early stages to call for social action. In Egypt, the government belatedly shut down the Internet and mobile phone networks but it soon became clear the horse had already bolted."[5]

The Internet might not be the source of social change, but as a medium it enables unrivaled momentum.

Just to be clear, your company doesn't have the option of shutting down the Internet to stop the spread of Social Influence.

If Social Influence can change a country, it can certainly change the way customers do business with – or decide to abandon – your company.

History teaches us that after a period of chaos, most countries (and people) do better with free markets and free will. In much the same way, we believe Social Influence is revolutionizing the relationship between customers and businesses. Ultimately, free markets and free choice will benefit all parties involved.

Don't think of Social Influence as a website or a place to advertise. Think of it as an unrelenting mirror reflecting the way your firm touches individual customers and your stakeholders in general. It's a mirror that will force changes within your culture and your processes, and it is in your interest to make such changes before the Social Influence mirror reveals your firm's flaws publicly.

We'll get into this in more detail later in the book, but let us point out now what you probably already know: the cultural changes required of your company are harder than the technological ones.

Much harder.

DISRUPTIVE FORCE NUMBER TWO: PERVASIVE MEMORY

Every time you use a digital device, you create a record of your actions.

These records, stored in databases around the world, document not only what is happening in your life, but also in the lives of most other people in the world. The more digital devices that exist, the more pervasive memory will become.

Of course, digital devices now surround us. When you walk through security in an office building or pass through a toll station in your car, digital devices create a record. Phones, video cameras, credit cards, passports, and cars create records every time you use them.

These records create a complex and comprehensive tapestry of our lives. They reveal where we go, with whom we interact, what we buy, when we buy, and how we buy.

Data reveals the truth.

Business has seldom revolved around the truth. At many firms, management makes decisions based on hunches or on imperfect data.

Companies had no reliable ways to know what customers really wanted, to understand how they made decisions, or even which products and advertisements were profitable.

Customer Relationship Management (CRM) was established as an industry to do just this. But it turned out that CRM is much better at automating sales processes and automating existing marketing functions than understanding customers.

The power of these four disruptive forces means that companies actually have the ability to track all this data for the first time: beyond what customers say they want, to what they truly want, by tracking what they do.

Not that most companies will do this, of course. Which leaves a huge opportunity – or a big challenge – for yours.

As a side effect of Pervasive Memory, firms will have access to vastly better – and more – information than ever before.

Companies will be able to monitor not only how individual customers behave, but also how their products perform. They will be able to spot and fix problems before they occur, by comparing the current status of a product to the expected status.

It is inevitable that companies will increasingly use such memories as a source of competitive advantage. Why? Because the greatest possible competitive advantage stems from having knowledge of customers that your competitors lack. If you understand what a customer likes, what they buy, when they buy, and how they buy, then you have a significant advantage.

Your competitive advantage is close at hand.

Think about it: Your competitor can duplicate your product quality, your prices and even your service levels. But if you have truly learned what makes one customer different from other customers, you have an advantage – assuming, of course, that you use this knowledge to better serve each customer.

The key to profitably using Pervasive Memory is to use it to benefit customers as well as your own firm.

You have to create win/win relationships. If you don't, you'll end up being attacked on social networks, criticized by bloggers, embarrassed by newspaper headlines, and in the very long run risk being sued by attorneys general as they struggle to keep up with the pace of technology advancements.

But let's consider for a moment what a company can do with Pervasive Memory when it's used to the customer's advantage.

You can anticipate their needs. You can operate in a way that saves them money and time. You can provide them with better products and better information. You can provide insights about both their work and personal life. You can connect them with other people, organizations, and events that will be of especially strong interest to them.

> **"IF TWO COMPANIES USE DATA WITH THE SAME EFFECTIVENESS BUT ONE CAN HANDLE 15% OF AVAILABLE DATA AND ONE IS STUCK AT 5%, WHO DO YOU THINK WILL WIN?"**
> — BRIAN HOPKINS, FORRESTER RESEARCH INC. ANALYST

History shows that most companies – how shall we put it? – miserably fail in using a customer's data to benefit the customer.

This fact has given rise to initiatives such as The Locker Project, an open source effort to collect an individual's "data exhaust" in one place and then motivate developers to build apps on top of this data. The goal is to benefit the individual, and to give the individual control over his or her data.

Kaliyah Hamlin, Executive Director of the Personal Data Ecosystem Collaborative Consortium, is optimistic about The Locker Project.

She observes, "A nascent but growing industry of personal data storage services is emerging. These strive to allow individuals to collect their own personal data to manage it and then give permissioned access to their digital footprint to the business and services they choose – businesses they trust to provide better customization, more relevant search results, and real value for the user from their data."[6]

The stakes are pretty clear. And pretty high.

Either established firms leverage Pervasive Memory to benefit individual customers, or there's plenty of money to be made by new players who will do this on behalf of those customers.

HEAVY METAL? NOT SO HEAVY ANYMORE...

One day, sensors will literally be floating in the air around us, and they'll be made of a metal like this. It's 99.9 percent air, and stronger than you might think.

It has a "micro-lattice" cellular architecture, which, as one UC Irvine researcher who worked on the project observed, actually gets stronger as dimensions are reduced to the nanoscale level. And it's light enough to sit on a dandelion without harming it.

Developments like this challenge old assumptions like "metal = heavy." And they make our disrupted future feasible.

DISRUPTIVE FORCE NUMBER THREE: DIGITAL SENSORS

The number of devices that are sensing our environment and then enabling a response is increasing exponentially.

When we talk about sensors, we mean everything from microphones and cameras to the dozens of devices that monitor the world around us (see Page 73).

Most of them are being leveraged to let devices – and firms – behave more intelligently. Because of the data they can generate, digital sensors go hand in hand with Pervasive Memory.

Today, sensors can measure just about anything.

Some measure pressure changes, others the presence of a chemical, and others changes in temperature. Sensors used to be largely present in factories and automated settings, but in recent years they have proliferated everywhere. Sensors went digital, shrank in size, and their power needs keep shrinking, which makes them more versatile.

Some sensors can now harvest energy from the environment, enabling uses in situations where it would be difficult or impossible to maintain a power supply. This would include monitoring bridge vibrations in certain critical but dangerous-to-reach and difficult-to-install locations.

Microsoft Kinect for Xbox 360 shipped eight-million units during its first two months on the market.[7] "You are the controller," announces Microsoft's ads, since Kinect learns to recognize each game player and uses your words and motions to control each game.

Kinect is a wonderful example of how sensors can both drive innovation and change customer expectations.

David Pogue, tech guru of the *New York Times* wrote:

> "It has four microphones and three little lenses: a video camera, an infrared projector and a distance sensor. Together, these lenses determine where you are in the room. And not just you.
>
> The system tracks 48 parts of your body in three-dimensional space. It doesn't just know where your hand is, like the Wii. No, the Kinect tracks the motion of your head, hands, torso, waist, knees, feet and so on...
>
> It doesn't merely recognize that someone is there; it recognizes your face and body. In some games, you can jump in to take a buddy's place; the game instantly notices the change and signs you in under your own name.
>
> If you leave the room, it pauses the game automatically."[8]

As result, Kinect will force companies in other industries to jettison controllers and develop products that can behave as intelligently as Kinect (dumber than a video game is not an effective long-term corporate strategy).

Within days, an Open Kinect group formed online and individuals started collaborating to develop open source code and strategies for hacking Kinect's capabilities.

Sensors are spreading into virtually everything.

From our digital devices to things we don't think of as being digital devices, like clothing and walls, the flood of innovation unleashed by sensors is already changing entire industries.

For example, UBM Techinsights recently warned the consumer medical device industry that:

> "The core elements of many personal medical devices – including processors, displays, memory, keyboard/data-entry methods, battery power, connectivity methods, speaker/headphones, and sensors – are being found increasingly in smartphones. Driven by apps, video, and gaming, smartphones have also become more sophisticated, boasting greater processing power and better sensors.

> As a result, electronics designers can now deliver valuable medical device functionality at a lower marginal cost through integration with smartphones. Lower prices to consumers who already possess smartphones increase the addressable market for integrated products as compared to more expensive, stand-alone medical devices."[9]

Says Jeff Brown, UBM's Vice President of Business Intelligence, "Smartphones provide medical technology companies with unprecedented access to an enormous consumer market.[10]

To capture this opportunity, they must think carefully about how they develop new technologies and protect their intellectual property innovations. Otherwise, they face the same fate as makers of stand-alone GPS and MP3 players – a slow decline to obsolescence."

In other words, smart customers can now tap into sensor networks that used to be available mainly through large, established firms who were often using proprietary systems.

How will sensors disrupt your industry or your business model? (It's a question of when, not if.)

These days, a wind sensor on a buoy outside of your town can tell you whether it's worth driving five miles to take your sailboat out or to go wind surfing. (It can also tell you whether the wind is increasing so much that you might want to tie down the furniture in your back yard.) You can determine this from your house or while on a business trip 3,000 miles away.

We used to think about digital technologies as (basically) computers, but now we recognize that they include a much broader range of devices, such as digital sensors, every camera, and every microphone or recording device.

We are burying sensors in our gardens, embedding them in our bridges and roads; they are floating on the seas and sometimes in the air. They are being used in warfare and research. Each creates more data, more information, and more opportunities for innovation.

Categories of Sensors

The categories at right were taken from the sensors section of *Sensors Magazine Buyer's Guide*, including more than 35,000 manufacturers of sensors...not including emerging categories of sensors.[11]

Acceleration

Acoustic and Audio

Chemical

Density and Specific Gravity

Displacement

Electrical and Electromagnetic

Encoders and Resolvers

Environmental

Flow

Force

Gas

Humidity and Moisture

Level

Linear Position

Orientation Position

Pressure

Proximity or Presence

Rotary Position

Safety Sensors/ Switches

Security Sensors/ Switches

Temperature

Tension

Tilt

Torque

Vacuum

Velocity

Vibration

Viscosity

Vision

Weather

TODAY, DIGITAL SENSORS CAN: MONITOR YOUR TIRE PRESSURE AND AVOID DANGEROUS BLOWOUTS; ANALYZE THE GAIT OF ELDERLY CITIZENS AND WARN OF FALLS BEFORE THEY OCCUR; FOLLOW THE GAZE OF SHOPPERS AND IDENTIFY WHICH PRODUCTS THEY EXAMINE – BUT DON'T BUY – IN A STORE; MONITOR WHICH PAGES READERS OF A MAGAZINE READ OR SKIP; FLOAT IN THE AIR OVER A FACTORY AND INDEPENDENTLY MONITOR THE PLANT'S EMISSIONS; DETECT IMPACTS IN THE HELMET OF AN ATHLETE AND MAKE IT IMPOSSIBLE FOR THEM TO HIDE POTENTIAL SERIOUS BLOWS TO THEIR BRAINS; REVEAL WHEN A DISHWASHER, REFRIGERATOR, COMPUTER, BRIDGE, OR DAM IS ABOUT TO FAIL; TRIGGER A DIFFERENT PROMOTION AS A NEW CUSTOMER WALKS BY A MESSAGE BOARD; ANALYZE THE DURATION AND QUALITY OF YOUR SLEEP; WARN DRIVERS THAT THEY ARE ABOUT TO FALL ASLEEP; PREVENT INTOXICATED DRIVERS FROM OPERATING A MOTOR VEHICLE; WARN A PERSON BEFORE HE OR SHE HAS A HEART ATTACK; DETECT WASTED ENERGY IN BOTH HOMES AND COMMERCIAL BUILDINGS; WARN A PARENT OR BOSS WHEN ANGER IS CREEPING INTO THEIR VOICE, TO HELP PREVENT THEM FROM SAYING OR DOING THINGS THEY WILL LATER REGRET; TELL WAITING CUSTOMERS HOW FAR AWAY THE PIZZA DELIVERY GUY IS FROM THEIR HOUSE; ANALYZE THE MOVEMENTS OF EMPLOYEES THROUGH A FACTORY TO DETECT WASTED TIME AND EFFORTS; TRIGGER PRODUCT DEMONSTRATIONS OR INTERACTIVE MANUALS WHEN A CUSTOMER PICKS UP OR EXAMINES A PRODUCT; CONGRATULATE AN ATHLETE WHEN SHE SWINGS A TENNIS RACQUET PROPERLY OR ACHIEVES AN EFFICIENT STRIDE WHILE RUNNING. **WHAT CAN THEY DO TOMORROW?**

DIGITAL SENSORS GO HAND IN GLOVE WITH PERVASIVE MEMORY BECAUSE EACH ONE OF THESE SENSORS GENERATES BIG DATA IN BIG DATABASES.

Truth is, we could fill the whole book with potential sensor uses. There are trillions of sensors in use already, and they will increasingly be used in wireless networks to help us make sense of the world around us.

Sensors create never-before-seen opportunities to drive value, change business models, and serve customers.

As a result, your company can introduce products and services that were not conceivable five years ago. Now, they're not just possible, they're practical. A retail store could recognize and greet customers as they enter the store; not a clerk, mind you – the store itself. That same store can monitor the paths shoppers take through the store, learning to adjust displays and product placements to maximize sales.

Let's say this again, because it's pretty important: a physical store can be just as smart or smarter than a website. So can an office building, or a dealer's showroom. We don't think of "bricks and mortar" as possessing this sort of intelligence, but with each passing day there are fewer reasons why not.

In our homes and offices, and in the world we pass through on a daily basis, we will be able to talk and/or gesture to the objects around us. The road there may be bumpy, but everything around us is going to get smarter.

Everything.

DISRUPTIVE FORCE NUMBER FOUR: THE PHYSICAL WEB

It doesn't take much foresight to recognize that we are already starting to hyperlink the physical world like we have the Web.

We use the term "Physical Web" here instead of Internet of Things, because the Physical Web will link everything, not just things to other things. People, animals, plants, and places will be as linkable as sensors, cameras, and computers.

Others will attach data to you, for example. When you walk into a room, other people will be prompted to remember information about your preferences, performance, and personality. Dramatic changes are coming, and at present we see a mere glimpse of what is to come.

Today – if you have the right phone or camera – you can use "augmented reality" applications to get information that is linked to physical objects and entities.

Point your phone down a suburban street and you will see which houses are for sale. Turn it toward the village center and you can see the direction of each restaurant, along with reviews for each. The award-winning astronomy app StarWalk turns an iPad into a magical tool for stargazers, identifying any constellation when you point the iPad in its direction.

Imagine you are traveling in Spain and don't speak Spanish. The Word Lens app lets you point your phone at any sign or printed page, and it replaces all the Spanish words with English ones.

This is so effective it's almost creepy; you still see the sign, but the words you can understand replace the ones you cannot.

In the near future, expect increased power and precision. Instead of locating the best hotel for your needs, you'll be able to identify the best available room in that hotel.

As you make new discoveries in the real world, you will be able to bookmark them.

If you are hiking deep in the woods and discover a beautiful clearing under a giant oak tree, you can bookmark it so you can easily find it on your next visit.

The SoundHound app lets you identify any song you hear playing, even if it's simply being sung by a kid on a street corner. Microsoft Tag and Google Goggles both allow companies to tag products so that customers can simply scan a code and see whatever information, demonstrations, or offers the company chooses to attach.

Such elements can be changed in real time, to enable timely offers, or to accommodate shifting inventories. Think of a blouse with such a tag; the attached offer could promote 50 percent off a matching skirt, until that skirt is sold out and the offer immediately shifts to promote a different accessory.

For the 2011 Super Bowl, *USAToday* joined forces with the Junaio augmented reality app to let individuals "stand" on the field and take a 360-degree tour of Dallas' Cowboys Stadium just by moving their smartphone in any direction.

UpNext offers 3D maps of major American cities, which let you zoom in on any section, block, or building. This app lets you immediately get a sense of distance between locations, or simply learn what the building you're headed toward looks like.

If you are looking for a Vietnamese restaurant in a particular neighborhood or a fun attraction, UpNext highlights all the businesses that meet your criteria (including a contextual visual representation of the building they're in) and gives you a concise written summary of each. Thanks to integration with Foursquare, the app can also help you find nearby places where your friends are currently gathering.

Trapster is an app that lets drivers alert each other about speed traps, enforcement cameras and road hazards. MSNBC called it "a community-based high-tech early warning system." iNap wakes train and subway riders before they pass their stop, because waking up in New Haven is a very jarring experience when you were headed for a morning meeting in Manhattan.

Get the idea?

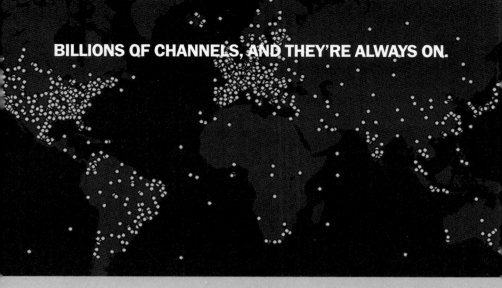

BILLIONS OF CHANNELS, AND THEY'RE ALWAYS ON.

THE PROGRAMMABLE WORLD

The picture above represents a very small slice of the Internet of Things. It's a snapshot of a handful of the devices feeding data to Cosm, a Web-based service "built to manage the world's real-time data" and give people "the power to share, collaborate, and make use of information generated from the world around them."

The devices represented above are embedded in consumer products, business environments, houses, factories, farms, roads, wine cellars and swimming pools, and attached to things like bridges, trees, sump pumps, computers, and generators.

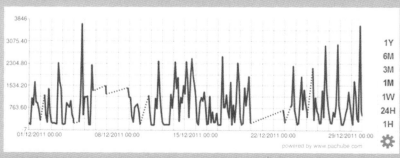

One month's electricity consumption: house in Sheffield, United Kingdom.

We are at the very early stages of tagging and linking the physical world, but that doesn't mean it's far in the future.

Much of the necessary technology already exists. It means that most corporate executives and business strategies have not yet recognized that the real world is being linked like the Web – but with more impactful consequences.

Why more impactful? Just think about what happens on the Web. Your movements can be tracked. Offers can be targeted to specific individuals. Genuinely helpful services such as Web banking replaced "free toaster" ads.

Nearly anything can be customized or personalized.

Physical Web technologies will solve small but frequent problems like losing your keys in your house, your car in a parking lot, or your kids outside playing.

It will also tackle huge problems like companies not really understanding which of their activities are profitable, which processes are broken, and which customers represent the future of their industry.

Linking the real world will allow both managers and individuals to take an increasingly granular view of the world, understanding what works and why.

As the Physical Web rises, pretty much everything a company does for its customers will become more interactive, dynamic, and open to scrutiny.

DISRUPTION FAVORS THE SMART CUSTOMER

These four forces add up to one word: smarter.

Everything around us is starting to act intelligently. From our appliances to our cars, our gardens to our watches, intelligent behavior is spreading. It's hard to overstate the scope of change this will produce.

Even in the dot-com era, when everyone and their neighbor was founding an Internet start-up, things didn't move as fast as they are moving now. Yes, it's much harder to launch a company; the economy stinks, at least in the first half of 2012, and funding is tight. But you don't even have to start a company to help drive the disruption that's happening now; you just have to create an app, and even high school kids are doing that. If enough "little guys" nip at the heels of large companies, it starts to create real pain.

Plus, the world is even flatter than it was a decade ago.

Kids in China, Russia, India, and Pakistan are competing with kids and even retirees in Cleveland and Detroit. Everyone is trying to figure this out, but in the meantime hundreds of new apps appear every day, and thousands of people buy smart new devices.

If a tree falls in the forest and no one is there to hear it, a sensor will hear the sound, detect the motion, and even measure the force of impact as it hits the ground. (See? Even life's tough questions will be answered soon.)

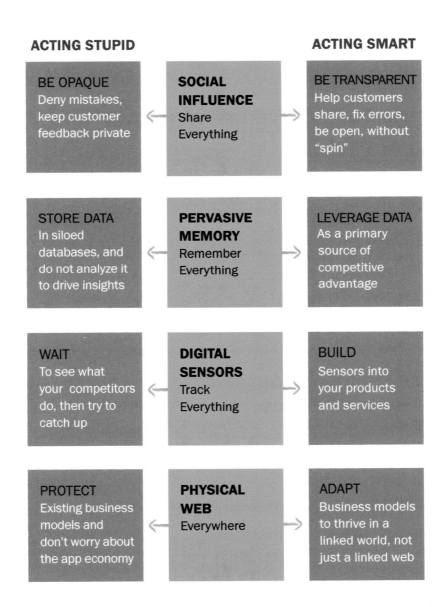

ACTING STUPID		ACTING SMART
BE OPAQUE Deny mistakes, keep customer feedback private	**SOCIAL INFLUENCE** Share Everything	**BE TRANSPARENT** Help customers share, fix errors, be open, without "spin"
STORE DATA In siloed databases, and do not analyze it to drive insights	**PERVASIVE MEMORY** Remember Everything	**LEVERAGE DATA** As a primary source of competitive advantage
WAIT To see what your competitors do, then try to catch up	**DIGITAL SENSORS** Track Everything	**BUILD** Sensors into your products and services
PROTECT Existing business models and don't worry about the app economy	**PHYSICAL WEB** Everywhere	**ADAPT** Business models to thrive in a linked world, not just a linked web

We are in the early stages of figuring out the ways that this "new world" really works.

People will walk around with cameras and microphones embedded in their glasses and clothing. These devices will record 24/7, and if something interesting happens, you can save the data.

You will be able to see the way you swing a baseball bat, carry yourself in school, conduct yourself in meetings, and interact with your spouse. Companies will monitor the way customers walk through their store, tracing not only physical paths but facial expressions, gestures, and perhaps even vital signs.

All of the data that is gathered, remembered, and analyzed can serve to make customers and companies smarter. The race is already on to make this vast and growing volume of data easily accessible as well as understandable.

As a result, we'll need ways to access insights as we move through the world. We're not sure whether this means glasses with "Terminator" type augmented displays, ads like those in "The Minority Report," or walls that function like monitors. The answer is probably "all of the above."

The end result will be smarter customers, and endless opportunities for businesses.

Your company will need to be able to entice and serve customers who never go anywhere without an expert at their shoulder.

This expert can guide your customer, no matter the subject or situation. How do you compete for the business of such customers?

By expert, of course, we mean instant remote access to insights from social networks, Digital Sensors, and Pervasive Memory (yes, customers will be able to tap into this treasure trove too) from wherever they are. These insights won't only be helpful online, they will also be invaluable in the "real" world, which will soon be as linked as the Web is now.

Customers will expect the same level of service whether it is 3 a.m. or 3 p.m. You will not be able to fool them by jacking up prices only to run a "fake" sale. You will not be able to hide a poor service record, or failure to provide professional support for your offerings.

Looking from the perspective of the status quo, this does sound pretty disruptive, doesn't it?

KEY TAKEAWAYS:

- Social Influence means companies will have less control over what customers think of their offerings, service, and reputation – because third parties will always be present in the relationship, even when firms sell direct.

- Pervasive Memory means that memory is everywhere, creating a marketplace (and society) in which the truth is nearly impossible to escape.

- Digital Sensors make possible "sense and respond" business models, in which companies respond intelligently to changes around both their customer and the world.

- The Physical Web is evolving as the real world gets linked much like the virtual world has, and the result is that we will browse, tag, and connect nearly everything.

- Together, these four disruptive forces create new business opportunities as they also undercut existing business models.

Four:
Stupid
Companies

DOES YOUR COMPANY BEHAVE STUPIDLY?

We'd like to suggest that you take a critical look in the mirror and answer what might be a difficult question: Does your company behave stupidly?

Sadly, most do. Not everywhere, not always. But asking the question means you'll learn where and how your interactions create or destroy customer value. Because the bigger question is: If your customers are getting smarter, how much longer can you get away with behaving stupidly?

With this understanding comes the ability to begin asking and answering the questions that can help your company embrace disruption, improve customer relationships, and leverage innovation to provide the right customer experiences at and through the most relevant touchpoints to the right customers.

After all, your company doesn't define customer experience. Customers do. Customer experience is based on how your customers perceive your organization and how well you meet their needs when they interact with, hear about, and do business with your company.

Yes, we are suggesting that companies improve experience any way possible. But we're also specifically advocating the pursuit and creation of smart, interconnected touchpoints as a core foundation of any customer experience improvement initiative.

But getting there won't be easy. There are too many companies with systems, processes, and perspectives ingrained in doing things the way they always have.

WHAT HAPPENS WHEN SMART CUSTOMERS MEET A STUPID COMPANY?

Most of the time, companies force customers to do business with them on their terms – carry their loyalty card, buy when they're open, and spend significant time repeating the most basic information: name, account numbers, passwords, and more, every time they transact on the Web, over the phone and in-person.

Employees don't have access to customer histories, much less their wants and needs, and – with a few notable exceptions, such as Amazon or Zappos – their websites don't remember what you've purchased, what you did, where you looked, or what interests you.

Customer experience feels broken.

Companies structured in operating silos with performance metrics and reward systems at odds with other departments deliver a customer experience that can be discordant at best, jarring and off-putting at worst.

From the customer perspective, it can be schizophrenic and annoying when the experience of working with the call center or a sales group is completely different from the experience of dealing with accounting, customer service, or installation.

Worse yet, it's stupid to be so obviously oblivious to your customers. They can tell that they're not seen as individuals, and that their wants and needs are neither addressed nor understood.

LARGE COMPANIES HAVE BEEN STRUGGLING
TO OVERCOME CUSTOMER SERVICE AND
DATA SILOS FOR DECADES, AND
THE PROBLEM IS BECOMING
A REAL THREAT TO THEIR
VERY EXISTENCE.

CALL
CENTER

RETAIL

SALES

WEB

The ways companies interact with their customers are not just stupid, they're often "dumb" as well.

By dumb, we mean that companies don't employ the technologies available to them (their "senses") to see, to hear, to learn from, and speak to their customers in an intelligent way.

Companies like this are not leveraging disruptive forces to build stronger relationships. They are not selling more products through real-time, crowdsourced data and opinion-gathering schemes. They are not giving customers what they want, when they want it.

A typically stupid company is much more likely to send a printed direct mail piece with an offering that's irrelevant, unwanted, and/or annoying to the 98 percent or more of customers that don't respond, in hopes of an incremental sale.[1]

Of course, it takes work for companies to figure out what the right messages and communications are for any given group of customers.

But what these stupid companies don't grasp is that the very real cost of sending irrelevant messages quickly reaches into the millions of dollars, as customers opt to have relationships with those companies that take the time to intelligently communicate and personalize their interactions.

So what happens when these smart, empowered customers interact with stupid companies in a free and open market?

The same thing that disruptive innovation has wrought on every market it impacts: change starts in pockets, coming from the edges of an industry, ultimately becoming a wave that threatens mainstream competitors.

From buggy whips and floppy disks to rotary phones and personal music players, unknowns become market leaders, while major players become minor players or disappear completely.

Today, the business of designing, creating, selling, and delivering products and services is changing forever – again. And those companies that continue to behave as they always have, run the risk of being as if they never were.

Every customer has his or her tales of woe in dealing with stupid companies. Yet this isn't a complete blind spot for all firms. Recognizing that the value of an enterprise flows almost entirely from its customers, companies have been trying to improve customer relationships for years, investing heavily in technology such as CRM, to do so.

WHY CRM HASN'T HELPED

Hint: R really does stand for relationship.

Customer Relationship Management (CRM) was originally developed as a way to improve customer experience, under the banner of an "IT-enabled business strategy focused on the development and maintenance of mutually beneficial relationships between the seller and his buyers."[2]

But it hasn't improved the customer experience much at all. The issue is simple: CRM doesn't actually track relationships or experiences, it tracks transactions. As a result, CRM doesn't take into account the customers' views of the company, and doesn't capture how these interactions make customers feel, much less what they want or need.

Yes, CRM does a great job tracking company perceptions of value, and tracking those interactions that are important to the company – sales, marketing, service, etc. – but it fundamentally misses what customers think, feel, and want as a result.

It delivers an inside-out perspective that means the conclusions reached by companies about customer relationships are skewed, based on the interactions that occurred rather than the customer perceptions that resulted.

While CRM can tell the company that two customers have the same set of interactions, it can't tell which customer is delighted, and which feels trapped, upset, and may be actively bad-mouthing the company online. This is important information.

Billions of dollars were invested in technology to deliver better customer experiences. So what happened?

Today, most CRM implementations are simply data stores of the company's view of the customer, corralling and distributing what a company knows about its customers while capturing – in some cases – individual customer interactions.

So you'd think that the billions of dollars invested in CRM each year would help companies avoid being so stupid. Add billions more in sales force automation (SFA), business intelligence (BI) and other enterprise-wide technologies to the mix, and you'd expect customer satisfaction and customer intelligence to skyrocket.

After all, in theory the combination of these technologies gives companies the ability to remember everything about their customers and their interactions, and give customers what they really need. Well, not really.

Why not? The answer is simple. Just because a company can remember "everything" by collecting more data doesn't mean they bother to use it.

The results are clear. Charting the American Consumer Satisfaction Index against worldwide investments in CRM software and services – which went from zero 15 years ago to nearly $15 billion in 2011 – the corresponding bump in satisfaction has been exactly zero.

TOUCHPOINTS:

CRM VIEW:

9.5.11:	9.5.11:	9.24.11:	9.24.11:
Ms. Consumer logs on to retail website	Size 6 red shoes purchased by Ms. Consumer from website	Order delivered to Ms. Consumer	Nothing tracked

CUSTOMER VIEW:

Great pictures on this website! I know just what the shoes I want look like, and they're $20 less than Zappos.	That was a pain. Why did I have to enter my personal info again? I've bought before – they should know me by now.	You've got be kidding! Size 5 green shoes?! Not as ordered. And I wanted to wear these tonight...	Why won't their mobile app let me change the order? I'll have to call tomorrow.

This is why customers get so upset.

People know that companies store their information. They get "targeted" direct mail at home and by email. They experience pop-up ads that try to sell them products they've been researching online as they surf the Internet from work or from home, and they get "friend" recommendations to connect with. "If companies can do this," they reason, "they should be able to use this information to help me."

In general, people are forgiving by nature. Even if a mistake is made, it's easy for customers to accept and be relatively happy – if not totally satisfied – with a genuine effort to serve them, as long as the mistake is a result of ignorance. ("I'm sorry, we didn't know you'd moved...let me fix that.")

9.25.11: Nothing tracked	9.26.11: Inbound call: Confirm product exchange	9.26.11: Emailed order confirmation and shipping cost estimate	9.27.11: Customer logs on to retail website: Size 6 red shoes order canceled
10 minutes fighting voice mail to find out customer service is closed Sunday? Really?	Finally! A real person. But why did I have to provide my account info twice?	Wait a minute – they screwed up, and are charging ME for shipping? Why didn't that guy tell me?	Last time I order from these idiots. I'll bet Zappos still has what I want...

But when the ability to provide a positive experience exists and a company doesn't bother to do so, the average customer gets justifiably infuriated.

It's hard for customers to forgive what are, to them, easily avoidable mistakes that should be quickly resolved.

> *"You're charging me a late fee on an invoice you sent to my old address? But you send marketing materials to my new address all the time – you obviously have it. What do you mean you won't reverse the charge? Come on...!"*

In addition to typically stupid "analog experiences" (rude sales people and the like) we believe that this issue is at the heart of growing customer dissatisfaction and soaring rates of customer disloyalty.

DOES THIS MEAN THE END OF LOYALTY?

In 2010, 82 percent of consumers said they'd stop doing business with a company after a bad customer experience. Not only is this an astonishingly high number, the 2009 number was up 27 percent from just four years prior.[3] Customer expectations are rising rapidly.

It's no coincidence that the number of customers willing to leave a company after a single bad experience has risen in near lock-step with the rates of broadband, social media, and smartphone adoption. Smart customers know what companies have access to, because in many cases they'll have access to that information as well.

They also know that the technology and the data exist to treat them intelligently. When companies don't do this, there are three obvious explanations:

- The company just doesn't care,
- They hold their customers in contempt, or
- They're just stupid.

In other words, the best case is ineptitude, the worst is willful disregard. Neither scenario sits well with smart, in fact with any, customers. Knowing that companies have the knowledge to treat them better – and don't – fuels negative emotions and drives customer perspectives in ways that no company can afford to ignore.

Yet companies continue to treat customers poorly. This is even true of large companies that theoretically have the resources to do much better.

In the real-time, application-driven economy, companies simply cannot afford to sit on this data. They need to aggregate, analyze, re-purpose, and use it to get, and keep, their customers engaged. And they'll need to do it faster and more efficiently than before, through every channel and mode of interaction including sales and marketing interactions, products, employees, stores, and websites.

Do you know what happens on the borderlines between you and your customers?

These interactions occur wherever your brand interacts with your customers, in the ever-shifting area between your company and those whose opinions (and money) are critical to your success. This territory – the "borderlines" that exist where companies interact with their customers – is where customer experience occurs.

This evolving ecosystem of potential interactions is where your customers are won and lost, where relationships blossom or wither, and where corporate reputations are made or dashed. As customers continue to get smarter, the type and number of possible interactions is quickly expanding towards seemingly infinite possibilities and dizzying complexity.

"WHAT'S IN IT FOR ME?"

Years ago when I was studying at Wharton, Dr. Charles Dwyer taught us his five-step system, How to Get Anybody to Do Anything You Want. It sounds Machiavellian, but isn't.

The system basically says you have to show people they will benefit by doing what you want.

So if you want your team to create a company that is more nimble, more responsive, and more profitable, you have to convince each person it will be in their interest to do so.

Dwyer says people think "that organizations are all about missions and visions and values and ideology and that they are all in it together and that they all believe the same thing...that is absolute counterproductive nonsense."

"Organizations are about individual human beings taking care of what is important to them," Dwyer says, explaining that we pretend that a company is an independent being, but it isn't.

Your company was created by people, is populated by people, and will act in a manner that those people determine for themselves.

As a company – or as an executive in your company charged with creating a more innovative, responsive firm – your job is to align what you need people to do with the reward systems that give them the incentive to do so.

— Bruce Kasanoff

MANY MANAGERS DON'T CARE – AND AREN'T PAID TO

Not long ago, Michael was in sunny south Florida interviewing the CEO of a $4 billion asset management group.

Bill, as we'll call him, runs a company that is one division of an integrated, multi-national financial services conglomerate with businesses across the Americas and Europe, and an initial foothold in Asia through a few strategic retail and commercial banking partnerships.

We don't have an "experience." We have a revenue stream.

The East Coast-based firm had recently hired us as part of an organization-wide customer experience improvement initiative.

Since understanding customer experience through the eyes of corporate leadership is an important step in improving it, we found ourselves across the desk from Bill in an expansive, well-appointed corner office on the 42nd floor of a marble-clad downtown high-rise.

Charming and smart, Bill is an Ivy-educated MBA in his mid-forties, about 15 years out of a major management consulting firm, in his third executive position since moving to the corporate side.

He got down to business pretty quickly.[4]

"Frankly, we're not even sure why you're here. 'Customer experience?' We don't have an 'experience.' We have a revenue stream," he said.

"My group services the loans sold by some of the other groups. Our job is to drive fee income from our portfolio of these loans. Our performance – heck, my compensation and that of my entire senior team – is based on how much money we generate from this portfolio. We drive revenue from interest fees, late fees, processing fees, and research fees."

He continued, "If I was to summarize our 'customer experience' in a phrase it would be this: 'We just don't care.' And why should we?

"There's no money in that. For our customers, a good experience means we don't charge them fees. Show me how I make money and collect fees, and then let's talk about experience."

We asked him what his customers might be worth to other groups.

"I don't know," he said. "But I don't really need to, do I?"

That's the problem in a nutshell. Many companies really don't care – other than how it relates to the self-interest of the employees charged with achieving goals on which their performance is measured.

At the same time, they don't have a clear understanding of what a customer is worth – either to other divisions or groups, or over the lifetime of the relationship.

As we illustrated earlier, this problem is also complicated by the silos that exist inside most companies. Silos break a few different ways. By business line or division, as in Bill's company, or by functional area, such as sales and service.

Many companies are siloed or break along both business or divisional and functional lines.

In some firms, marketing feels as if it owns the customer, and is often charged with gathering and analyzing voice of the customer (VoC) feedback, where oftentimes the resulting insights remain. CRM is the domain of IT and sales.

The Web has only recently become a shared channel for marketing and IT, while operations, customer service, and product development are often second in line when it comes to leveraging it. Contact center platforms tend to be separate from the rest of the enterprise, and every one of these groups has key performance metrics (KPIs) that they're judged by – and in many cases compensated on – that have little or no relation to their overall effect on the customer.

For customers, interacting with a company across channels and groups can be a difficult experience. The brand communicates one message, and marketing leverages this perception to attract customers. Sales works to close the deal, but sometimes legal or compliance jumps in and gets in the way with conflicting information.

Once logged in (or through cookies that detect previous behavior and serve up content based on that), the company website offers one view of the relationship, and one way to authenticate (password and email, usually). Then a call to the customer service center serves up different information, often requiring a totally different set of security protocols (Where were you born? What's your mother's maiden name? What are the last four of your social?) that feel invasive and annoying.

If a password and username is secure enough for the Web, why don't companies use this information at their call center also?

But we're doing the best we can!

A few pages ago we talked about how difficult it is for smart customers to forgive what appear to be obviously avoidable mistakes.

But when we've talked to people inside these companies – the employees charged with delivering "stellar customer service" through the touchpoints they control – this reaction can feel unfair. After all, they're doing the best they can with what they have. Every day it seems there's more to learn, less time to do it, and more demands for results.

Most of these employees don't have a single view of the customer, their enterprise systems are disconnected, and they have no idea that two other groups (or more) are engaged with that same customer at that same time, often on related issues.

SOCIAL SEGMENTATION?

The ability to understand customer differences is exploding in ways that were impossible just a few years ago. For example, several companies are working to build models and methodologies to help brands anticipate customer needs by segmenting them through the lens of Social Influence.

From co-creation agency Face in London, the picture above represents sub-communities with common areas of interest within two degrees of separation from a client's brand on Twitter.

In San Francisco, Whit.li mines Facebook data, giving companies the ability to immediately provide the "right" type of customer service for a given customer, rather than forcing all customers – say, both grandmothers and technical wizards – to go through the same set of online or voice mail prompts.

GUESS WHAT? YOUR CUSTOMERS DON'T CARE EITHER

They're not just taking money when they leave...

Your company's issues are of no concern to most of your customers. They have a choice, which they're exercising with greater abandon than ever: simply go somewhere else.

On their way out your door, they're doing more than walking away with years of future revenue forever trapped in their wallets. These dissatisfied customers are going to tell their friends about it. Potentially thousands of them.

What pushes customers out the door?

Every time your company or your brand interacts with a customer – online and off, in-person or not, between or about your organization and any member of your audience universe – you "touch" them.

No matter where these touches occur or who initiates or controls them, we call these interactions touchpoints. Touchpoints encompass every possible type of interaction between a company and its customers.

For an airline, they might range from waiting areas, drink carts, in-flight refreshments, flight attendants, and in-flight entertainment systems to travel agents, television and radio advertisements, customer service centers, mileage statements, credit card offers, websites, text messages, and more.

For a technology company, touchpoints might include things like salespeople, websites, invoicing, call-center based help desk, product packaging and documentation, online chat, direct mail or print advertising, third-party distributors, warranty cards, store displays, and even the actual product.

In a hospital, admitted patients receive over 100 "touches" during a typical day, from blood pressure reading and temperature taking to meal delivery and doctor visits. Starting with the admissions desk and insurance forms, touchpoints can include radiology, orderlies, and the warmed blanket that some patients get while waiting for a procedure, or a room. The room itself is a touchpoint, too.

Depending on how well it meets customer needs and expectations, each touchpoint either brings customers closer to you, or helps to push them out the door.

Do you know what your touchpoints are?

Your industry has a common set of touchpoints that most customers encounter; your business specifically has many more, which together create, define, and deliver the unique experience of working with your company.

Customer perceptions of and attitudes around individual companies are driven by the combined experiences delivered through their touchpoints.

JUST THREE KINDS OF TOUCHPOINTS DELIVER CUSTOMER EXPERIENCE

STATIC	**HUMAN**	**DIGITAL**

STATIC	HUMAN	DIGITAL
Static touchpoints allow information to flow one way: from the touchpoint to the customer. Customers have to take action.	Human touchpoints allow information to flow two ways, through "voice-to-voice" conversation, either in person, online, or by phone.	Digital touchpoints are interactive, and allow information to flow any way. Companies and customers interact on an ongoing basis.

They can include:

▪ Products	▪ Sales Reps	▪ Phone Apps
▪ Retail Stores	▪ Call Center	▪ Corporate Web
▪ Newsletters	▪ Service Personnel	▪ Tablet Apps
▪ Coupons	▪ Industry Experts	▪ Social Media
▪ Print Ads	▪ Angry Customers	▪ Twitter
▪ Packaging	▪ Retail Clerks	▪ Extranets
▪ Billboards	▪ Delivery Drivers	▪ Competitor Blogs
▪ Media Articles	▪ Competitors' Staff	▪ Online Reviews
▪ Direct Mail	▪ Speeches	▪ Facebook
▪ Flyers	▪ Receptionists	▪ Corporate Blogs
▪ Invoices	▪ A/R Staff	▪ Sensors
▪ Magazines	▪ Happy Customers	▪ IVR System
▪ Postcards	▪ Support Staff	▪ M2M Devices
▪ Radio Ads	▪ Installation	▪ Product Web

Effective touchpoints move customers closer to a company, ineffective touchpoints push customers away.

Customer experience is the perception that customers have of their interactions with an organization. Another way to put it is this: the sum of a company's touchpoints equals the customer experience.

But customer experiences are not just driven by touchpoints that your company controls. In the world of disruptive forces, touchpoints which you own but don't always control – data (accessed by others), pricing, hours of operation, and inventory levels, to name a few – can also drive customer experience.

In addition, many touchpoints which have a profound influence on customer experience are outside your direct control. Like word-of-mouth, bloggers and the media, distributors, resellers, retailers, outsourced customer service, or marketing partners who sell under your good name, all "touch" your customers.

Of course, this discussion of touchpoints doesn't capture the way that customers "feel" after interacting with them. How do their current beliefs and attitudes affect customer perceptions of a touchpoint? Do they address the wants and needs that exist at any given point of time during the relationship? Do they engender customer confidence, indifference, or loathing?

In short, every touchpoint creates an impression of your company at the point where your brand touches your audience.

DUMB TOUCHPOINTS ANCHOR YOUR PERFORMANCE TO THE PAST

By now it will come as no surprise. Touchpoints are increasingly interactive, and smarter.

As with the many technological innovations that came before, the mobile Web and the ever-connected customers that access it are driving a dramatic shift in the roles, types, and functionality of touchpoints.

As customers and companies use technology to share what they and their customers and employees do, buy, think, and watch, the importance of touchpoints getting smarter, faster, and more relevant increases daily.

We're already seeing smart touchpoints everywhere. For example, irrigation controls are changing the way landscaping is managed, by changing the amount of water released through sprinkler systems based on numerous near-real-time inputs including soil and atmospheric moisture content, historical weather patterns, and national weather service forecasts.

Wireless-device-based shopping apps let customers instantly compare, and in many instances purchase, alternative products (or the same products at a lower cost) in a retail environment. "Smart tags" allow companies and people to append any amount or type of data they wish to almost any physical object or place.

But this doesn't change the fact that most companies still have too many static and "dumb" touchpoints.

THE FUTURE IN A BLUE SQUARE

In the words of inventors John Kestner and David Carr, "Twine is the simplest possible way to get the objects in your life texting, tweeting or emailing. A durable 2.5" square provides WiFi connectivity, internal and external sensors, and two AAA batteries that keep it running for months. A simple Web app allows you to quickly set up your Twine with human-friendly rules — no programming needed."[5]

Want a text when your laundry is done? Put Twine on top of your dryer, and tell Twine to text you. Want to know when your back door opens? Use Twine.

Bruce pitched in $165 to support Twine on Kickstarter, where individuals can fund creative projects. The day he heard about it, Michael did the same thing, joining the 3,965 other backers who eventually pledged over $556,541 versus the $35,000 David and John were initially seeking.[6]

Kickstarter is a great way to not only fund a project, but also to assess market potential. Unlike some market research efforts that ask (theoretically) how interested you would be in a new product, Kickstarter requires you to spend actual money on the new idea. That's the best test of all.

There are so many things we love about this. It will enable all of us to figure out innovative uses for sensors without knowing programming. And it demonstrates how entrepreneurs with an idea can bypass traditional investors, friends, and family to raise money.

"IT ISN'T THE INCOMPETENT WHO DESTROY AN ORGANIZATION. THE INCOMPETENT NEVER GET IN A POSITION TO DESTROY IT. IT IS THOSE WHO ACHIEVED SOMETHING AND WANT TO REST UPON THEIR ACHIEVEMENTS WHO ARE FOREVER CLOGGING THINGS UP." — F. M. YOUNG, AUTHOR

Dumb touchpoints are those that can't understand a customer's needs or gather data about their actions. While they have a place, dumb touchpoints tend to deliver too little value to their customers, and cost too much.

Consider the cost of planning, developing, printing, and distributing a simple letter to thousands of customers on an ongoing basis, versus the cost of a targeted email. Or a printed annual report versus an interactive one that allows investors to dig in (and allows companies to learn what customers are interested in digging into).

Stupid touchpoints are usually dumb touchpoints that are also unimportant to customers, and/or ineffective at achieving their desired goals. Unfortunately, most companies have no idea if their touchpoints are just dumb, or dumb and stupid. It's not a difficult task to find out, and the companies that do so nearly always learn things that surprise them and generate significant value.

One example of how making dumb touchpoints smart saved millions, and made for much happier customers.

We worked with a large telecom that was trying to improve the "first 60 days satisfaction" of small business DSL customers. From an initially high rating a few days after installation, the number dropped precipitously over the next couple months.

The customers themselves helped us figure out the problem.

Of the 47 touchpoints the average customer encountered – ranging from static direct mail and human installers to interactive online registration – it turned out that one thing was really ticking these customers off.

Sitting in their truck, each technician sent each customer his or her own network passcode via secure email immediately following installation. This wasn't the problem.

The problem was the confirmation letter mailed by the company a few weeks later, containing the same network passcode. "Since we're sending the letter anyhow," someone reasoned, "let's tell these new customers about all the other products and services we have to offer."

From the company perspective they were leveraging one touchpoint to communicate several messages. However, the customer perspective was different. "I can't believe this company is sending my private data through the mail!" was a common reaction. "And they're doing so as a transparent excuse to sell me more things I don't want or need!"

This "dumb" touchpoint was ineffective and redundant – actively driving negative customer perceptions at a fully-loaded annual cost of about $1.5 million. The solution was simple. By eliminating this touchpoint – essentially converting a "dumb" touchpoint to a "smart" touchpoint that already existed – this telecom was on track to save $15 million over 10 years, improving customer satisfaction in the process.

KINECT FOR XBOX 360 HAS SENSORS THAT HAVE THE ABILITY TO SEE AND LISTEN TO YOU, INTERPRETING AND RESPONDING TO YOUR GESTURES AND COMMANDS.

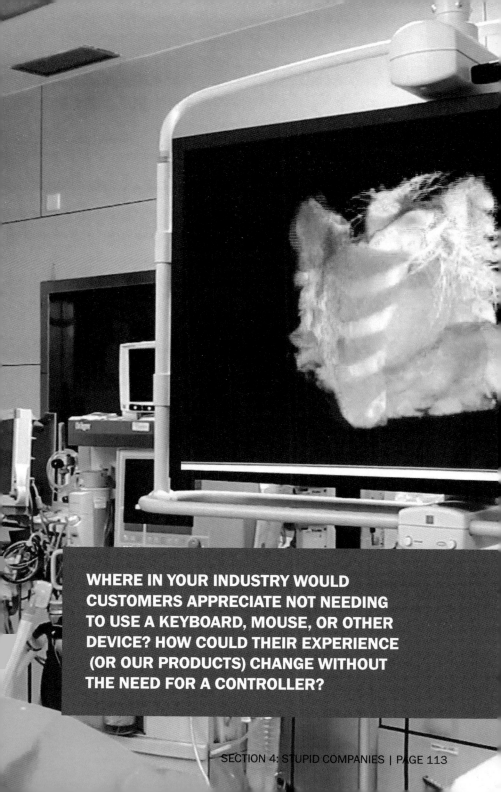

WHERE IN YOUR INDUSTRY WOULD CUSTOMERS APPRECIATE NOT NEEDING TO USE A KEYBOARD, MOUSE, OR OTHER DEVICE? HOW COULD THEIR EXPERIENCE (OR OUR PRODUCTS) CHANGE WITHOUT THE NEED FOR A CONTROLLER?

The end result of these changes is inevitable: Touchpoints (and customers) are getting smarter.

As digital touchpoints continue to grow, the number of touchpoints a customer encounters as they move through your relationship lifecycle is moving towards the potentially infinite.

As customers move from one channel to the next (store to website to call center to website to IVR system to checkout – all while in your physical store) your touchpoints and the systems that deliver them will need to seamlessly hand off from channel to channel.

At the same time, your touchpoints and the systems gathering and acting on the data they create can (and should) work together to create ever smarter and more personalized interactions.

Bottom line? Your customers and their expectations of experience are changing. Your touchpoints should be changing too.

The question isn't whether or not you should convert static touchpoints to smart touchpoints. (You should.)

It's prioritizing which touchpoints you should convert, and moving as quickly as possible on those that are most important.

The end result of these trends is inevitable: touchpoints are getting smarter, and there are LOTS more of them.

Yesterday:

Just a few years ago, most touchpoints were still static. Print ads, direct mail, point-of-purchase displays, etc. were the primary method of reaching customers. Even as the Web gained significance, it was hard to for companies to make the shift to digital interactions.

Today:

New smart touchpoints driven by social media, mobile apps, and easy access to data are helping the type and number of interactions between customers and companies to multiply dramatically. The lines defining traditional communications and distribution models have become increasingly hazy.

Tomorrow:

Touchpoints will continue to get smarter just as they will continue to expand exponentially. Companies will have the ability to leverage "sense and respond" touchpoints to better manage relationships, supply chains, and distribution. Smarter, faster, and more effective touchpoints become more feasible.

As a result, the ability to create direct connections between your customers and your company through smart touchpoints creates significant opportunities, and provides critical competitive advantages.

By building smart touchpoints right into products and services, companies can create direct connections between themselves and their customers, actively controlling or influencing the customer experience.

Opportunities abound to design smart and interconnected products and services, providing the kind of information companies need to actively understand, measure, and improve customer experience across all their touchpoints.

This means eliminating as many dumb touchpoints as possible (and eliminating all stupid touchpoints), making static touchpoints smarter, human touchpoints interactive, and interactive touchpoints intelligent.

Nest is one of the first learning devices about to populate our homes and offices. Turn it on, and it learns your preferences: when you need the room warmer, and when it's OK to let things cool down a bit. It's also one of the first everyday, "boring" objects infused with an Apple-like design sense. Expect many, many more.

KEY TAKEAWAYS:

- In large numbers, customers perceive that many companies are inflexible, unresponsive, and/or generally unhelpful.

- CRM hasn't helped, because most CRM projects still look at things from the company's perspective, not the customers'.

- In many firms, employees are not rewarded for fostering customer loyalty.

- Smart companies will require smart touchpoints, which are interactive rather than static.

- Smart touchpoints have the potential to create highly profitable new services, and competitive advantages, for your company.

Five:
Get Smart

A FIVE-STEP SYSTEM FOR ACTING SMART AND GROWING FASTER

There are myriad reasons that companies behave stupidly when interacting with customers.

For some, it's simply a lack of desire or ability. For others, the systems aren't in place to behave intelligently. Failures can, and do, occur everywhere.

Companies that lack a process or framework to address the forces we describe often find themselves in reactive mode, or addressing them at a siloed level.

Let's imagine your CEO is convinced that to be competitive in the years ahead, your firm must use customer experience as a differentiator. You have one month to create a master plan that will accomplish this.

The CEO is also a no-nonsense, results-oriented leader with no tolerance for plans that take more than 60 seconds to summarize. How do you balance her need for simplicity with the overwhelming complexity of customer experience systems and strategies?

Implement a framework for getting SMART.

We understand that no one system fits every company, but what we offer here is an approach that will help most companies move quickly in the right strategic direction.

On the pages that follow, we lay out a framework that will point the way for any company to get, and continue to act, smart when dealing with their most assuredly smart customers.

GETTING SMART: A SIMPLE SYSTEM YOU CAN USE

You can't just install "smart."

In addition to being a framework, acting smart is an organizational mindset, a way of thinking, and an ongoing system of capabilities comprised of the following five steps:

1. Segment your customers by needs and value.

2. Modularize products, services, processes, and capabilities to increase flexibility and responsiveness.

3. Anticipate customer needs.

4. Reward your employees for win/win behaviors.

5. Transform touchpoints by making them smart.

Balancing a need for simplicity with the overwhelming complexity of customer experience systems and strategies.

SMART provides the lenses you need to assess opportunity and act intelligently, methodically, and confidently in response to the fast-paced, continually evolving complexity of smart customers, disruptive technologies, and potentially infinite touchpoints.

Taken together, these five steps will help you create a nimble and responsive organization...one designed around customer needs, as well as one that remains in close contact with individual customers – driving value as a result.

In summary, SMART will help you drive business success in the age of digital disruption. Let's take a closer look at each step.

Anytime Access	Looking for Help, Looking for Information, and Transacting	Anywhere Access

SMART
CUSTOMERS

S M A R T

SEGMENT customers by needs and value

MODULARIZE products and capabilities

ANTICIPATE the needs of customers

REWARD employees for win/win behaviors

TRANSFORM touchpoints, and make them smart

DISRUPTIVE
FORCES

Social Influence	Pervasive Memory	Digital Sensors	Physical Web

SEGMENT YOUR CUSTOMERS BY NEEDS AND VALUE

Understanding your customers at a granular level is key to serving them, and to making a profit while doing so.

One of the most common barriers to being intelligent about customer experience is lack of customer knowledge or understanding. When we talk about segments based on this, we're talking about looking through two primary lenses:

- Needs: What they actually want, need, and expect from you;

- Value: What your customers are or may be worth to your firm.

When most companies talk about segmenting customers, they mean segmenting by value. They divide customers into segments based on actual or potential sales. They strive to understand how much revenue they could get from a given group of customers.

Value segmentation is important from the company's perspective; it helps your company know on which customers it makes sense to focus efforts. It also points towards groups that might be better served with a lower-touch, lower-cost, digital strategy.

It's an important first step. But most companies stop here. You cannot afford to. Why? It doesn't help you understand what one customer needs versus another.

The bottom line is that if you don't segment customers by their individual needs, it will be incredibly difficult to deliver exceptional customer experience or to remain competitive.

SEGMENT TO DRIVE GREATER CUSTOMER VALUE

Application of customer segmentation drives enterprise value in these four areas: i) Financial value, measured by increased revenue and profitability; ii) Customer acquisition efforts; iii) Customer loyalty and retention; iv) Competitive advantage, driven by your ability both to "act smart" and "see" into the future to predict customer behavior and anticipate customer needs.

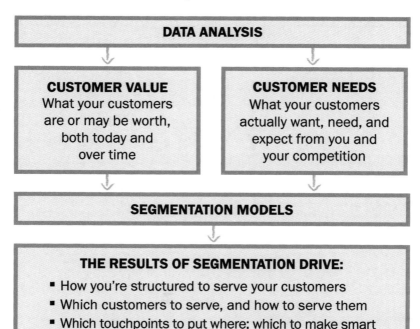

DATA ANALYSIS

CUSTOMER VALUE
What your customers are or may be worth, both today and over time

CUSTOMER NEEDS
What your customers actually want, need, and expect from you and your competition

SEGMENTATION MODELS

THE RESULTS OF SEGMENTATION DRIVE:
- How you're structured to serve your customers
- Which customers to serve, and how to serve them
- Which touchpoints to put where; which to make smart
- What experiences to deliver, and to whom

Without a definitive understanding of your customers, everyone in your company is essentially flying blind when it comes to delivering good customer experiences.

Unfortunately, many companies don't look at customers this way. Or, if they do, they often don't share the information effectively across other silos and groups internally.

Not knowing your customers in this way means that you will consistently fail to give your customers what they want at any given point, virtually ensuring that you will deliver sub-par experiences at least some of the time no matter how well you do everything else.

This also means that you will fail to grasp opportunities to satisfy or delight them, and will also miss otherwise obvious opportunities to increase customer value.

Segmentation is the engine for driving smarter customer experiences.

Just as importantly, defining your customers by value and needs on a segment-by-segment basis provides a highly efficient lens through which to make your touchpoints smarter.

It provides the framework for a methodical approach to leveraging the massive amounts of data almost every organization of scale gathers on its customers as a result of the electronic breadcrumbs scattered by each of us as we interact through digital channels such as the Web and our phones.

"TO CHANGE YOUR RETURN-ON-CUSTOMER, YOUR COMPANY WILL HAVE TO INTERACT WITH HIM IN A WAY THAT IS INFLUENCED NOT JUST BY YOUR KNOWLEDGE OF HIS VALUE, BUT ALSO BY YOUR INSIGHT INTO HIS INDIVIDUAL NEEDS AND MOTIVATIONS."
— DON PEPPERS AND MARTHA ROGERS, *RETURN ON CUSTOMER*

Questions to ask:

- Do you know what your customers really want and need?

- Is there a shared understanding of who your most valuable customers are and how to meet their needs?

- Do you understand common needs that all your customers have? And the unique needs each segment has?

- Is your customer data integrated and easily accessible across your organization, or is it stuck in silos?

Steps you can take:

- Analyze and summarize the data and "digital breadcrumbs" customer relationships and smart touchpoints generate.

- Integrate "outside in" Voice-of-the-Customer (VoC) data.

- Use segmentation to predict customer behavior and needs.

- Reorganize business functions modularly, based on segmentation insights and customer needs.

Benefits your organization may expect:

- Significantly improve marketing and sales effectiveness.

- Empower employees to make decisions based on the value of customers, and to better address customer needs.

- Improve customer experience and strengthen relationships.

- Increase the lifetime value of customers.

MODULARIZE YOUR CAPABILITIES TO INCREASE YOUR FLEXIBILITY AND RESPONSIVENESS

Companies need the flexibility to accommodate the differences between customers.

They also need the flexibility to respond to change. These include changing customer needs, market dynamics, competitive threats, and other potentially fast-moving technologies, trends, and forces.

This is Apple leveraging customer-centric design skills for mobile computing. It's Amazon using their computing and distribution expertise to build new business units and provide services to competitors. It's apps and plug-ins, and making functional parts that play nice with other functional parts.

The way to do this is to develop modular capabilities that can adapt to these changing needs. While modular capabilities can and should exist across your organization, they tend to be most efficient at leveraging your unique assets in these three areas:

- Teams: Organized around talent and competencies;

- Processes: Designed to efficiently support your people, your products and services, and your customers;

- Products: Driving personalization and mass-customization.

In a world of disruptive change and colliding, overlapping markets, the ability to be flexible and responsive in this manner means the ability to thrive – and to do so as others become marginalized, wither, and die.

MODULARIZE YOUR TEAMS, PROCESSES AND PRODUCTS

Modularity gives an organization the capability to respond more profitably and intelligently to customer interactions, by becoming more responsive, flexible and efficient. Not only does modularity help a company better accommodate the differences between customers, it also improves the ability to respond to – and thrive – in the face of competitive threats and other external forces.

IDENTIFY AND CULTIVATE ELEMENTS THAT CAN BE REUSED IN NEW WAYS

TEAMS	**PROCESSES**	**PRODUCTS**
Help employees gain new skills, combined new ways	Develop reliable processes that have multiple applications	Use components that can be used in many products and services

WHEN PLANNING FOR NEW PROJECTS, COMBINE EXISTING ELEMENTS IN UNIQUE COMBINATIONS

MODULAR CAPABILITIES:
- Increase organizational flexibility and responsiveness
- Speed reaction to changing market dynamics
- Reduce cost and duration of product/service development
- Lower the cost of providing customization

What do modular capabilities look like?

By "modular capabilities," we mean utilizing components designed to play nice with others. To use a simple example, if you operate a Wordpress blog, you can choose from thousands of plugs-ins to add new capabilities to your blog. If you own a smartphone, you can quickly customize it by downloading a dozen apps, or perhaps eight dozen.

In a modular organization, modularity is gained by the manipulation and organization of people, processes, and the utilization of assets. This structure supports the delivery of modular, personalized, and mass-customized touchpoints of all types, including smart products, services, and experiences.

This modular mindset needs to pervade your organization, enabling you – or your customers – to mix and match as required to respond to changing or individual needs.

This isn't just a "nice to have." It's a "must have."

Modular capabilities make it both possible and profitable to meet increased customer expectations in the face of revolutionary technologies. Customization will become routine and cost-efficient as you tailor the way you treat and interact with your customers. Costs will go down, driven by lower delivery costs and the elimination of redundancies and waste. Revenue will go up, driven by greater customer loyalty, competitive differentiation, and higher margins.

"AM I AN OPTIMIST? OPTIMISM AND PESSIMISM ARE BESIDE THE POINT. THE KEY IS NOT TO PREDICT WHAT WILL HAPPEN, BUT TO HELP SHAPE THE FUTURE."
— STEVEN JOHNSON, AUTHOR

Questions to ask:

- What capabilities is your organization particularly adept at?

- Can you profitably provide personalized and/or customized products, services, and experiences?

- Can you define and bring offline capabilities online?

- Where can experiences be replicated to meet different needs at different lifecycle stages?

Steps you can take:

- Bring your customers into the design process early on.

- Look for opportunities to change the look and feel or function of your products, services, and experiences.

- Create cross-functional teams to identify core competencies.

- Look for opportunities to leverage digital technology to allow customers to personalize experiences or services.

Benefits your organization may expect include:

- The ability to deliver individualized customer experiences, driven by the preferences and needs of individual customers.

- Reduction in costs, driven by lower delivery costs and the elimination of redundancies and waste.

- Increased margins, through the delivery of differentiated products and services and increased customer loyalty.

DELL LISTENS TO ITS CUSTOMERS, AND GIVES THEM WHAT THEY NEED.

Without the inertia of most larger, established companies, smaller companies tend to be nimbler and more innovative. Yet when an enterprise "gets it" – such as Zappos, Amazon, USAA, and others – they dominate. Their markets are forever changed.

In the case of computer and technology company Dell, this means better understanding and getting closer to their customers than any competitor. Leveraging principals of the SMART framework, Dell has enjoyed myriad benefits, including:

- **Higher satisfaction:** Resolution rates of 99 percent;

- **Greater engagement:** 46 percent increase in customer reach, with the same number of employees;

- **More loyal customers:** 34 percent increase in customer champions, or promoters.

It starts with segmentation. Not just by monetary value, but through an understanding of customer wants and needs driven through behavioral and listening analytics.

Modularization means that the company's expertise at creating, listening to and interacting with social media content has been taught to over 5,000 employees across multiple geographies and business units through a regimented curriculum.

Analysis of customer data includes daily monitoring of over 22,000 online conversations in 11 languages, and using the resulting insights to make business decisions around things like marketing, product development, and customer service delivery.

Employees are rewarded for solving customer problems and delivering win/win experiences, more effectively – and very consciously – driving customers through the sales funnel.

Touchpoints are customized, in many cases, on-the-fly: Does your personality type respond better to an empathetic listener? Login to customer service through Facebook, and you'll likely be matched to the "right" kind of customer support personnel.

With "Dell Hell" – a classic case study of how NOT to deal with an upset customer in the then-new blogosphere – Dell had the dubious distinction of being one of the earliest and most publicly visible examples of how Social Influence can quickly decimate a company's reputation and enterprise value.

But Dell has learned. And you should too. Because chances are high that the ways they're driving value by listening to and engaging with customers across multiple touchpoints, channels, and journeys will soon be coming to your industry as well.

Someone's listening.

In a room like this, Dell's widely applauded Social Media Listening and Command Center (founded in December of 2010) was visited by over 300 businesses in the last year alone. It's a virtual Lourdes for enterprise organizations looking for ways to make their customer relationships healthier, and their customer experiences stronger.

ANTICIPATE YOUR CUSTOMERS' NEEDS

Anticipate the needs of your customers by understanding the data that increasingly surrounds them.

Whether you have 1,000, 10,000 or 10 million customers, every interaction they have with you leaves behind a trail of potentially valuable data.

This data is not limited to that generated by interactions with you. Opinion, commentary, and other unstructured and unsolicited data is also available across the social Web.

Even a few years ago, the resources required to store and analyze the massive volumes of data generated by your customers meant that large, established companies held the advantage. No more. In fact, the legacy systems that gather this data and store it in disconnected operational silos means the advantage has shifted to smaller or more nimble organizations.

With the ability to leverage massive amounts of complex customer data well within the reach of any firm, there is no excuse not to be smarter about the ways this data can inform strategy and decisions.

Even so, many established firms simply have not leveraged technology or shifted their organizational structures, business processes, or product lines in a manner that permits intelligent use of customer insights. Soon, it will be too late for companies such as these. Smart customers simply expect more.

UNDERSTAND DATA SURROUNDING YOUR CUSTOMERS

As a direct result of the forces we describe in this book, the ability to gather, interpret, and act on this data is within your reach, no matter the size or scale of your firm. Tying customer data into powerful "Business Intelligence" software can help you anticipate and respond intelligently to customer needs.

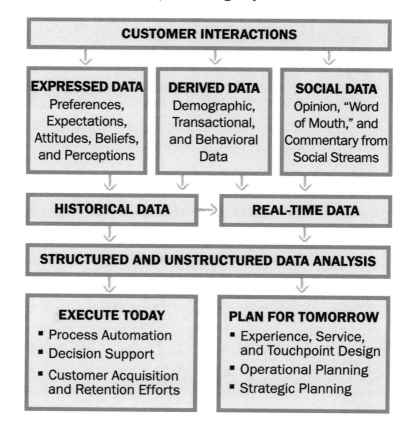

Pattern recognition is what intelligence is all about.

When you look at the data surrounding your customers – how and when they look for help, what they buy and how they use your services, for example – patterns and insights emerge.

You can identify patterns in your website usage, in customer service calls, in customer orders, and in product returns. By doing so, you start to actively predict what is going to happen next so you can anticipate what a customer is going to need in each step of the sales and service process.

Or better yet, you can use these insights to prevent annoying incidents from happening at all.

Most firms don't even make an effort to anticipate what the customer will do – or need – next. If you do, you can become dramatically more responsive in the customer's eyes.

How understanding data can help anticipate customer needs.

If you know something is going to happen a day, week, or month from now, or if you know your customer tried to find an answer but was unsuccessful, you can call that customer rather than making them reach out to you (or a competitor).

Intelligently interacting with a customer is the best way to get more business from them. The ability to use customer data to anticipate customer needs and intelligently respond is what will separate the firms that thrive from those firms that have no future at all.

"IT'S IMPOSSIBLE TO MOVE, TO LIVE, TO OPERATE AT ANY LEVEL WITHOUT LEAVING TRACES, BITS, SEEMINGLY MEANINGLESS FRAGMENTS OF PERSONAL INFORMATION."
— WILLIAM GIBSON, FUTURIST AND AUTHOR

Questions to ask:

- Are you learning from the customer data generated by your current digital relationships?

- Do you have a unified (cross-channel and cross-functional) repository of "customer intelligence" data?

- Can you respond intelligently to customer actions?

Steps you can take:

- Identify existing repositories of customer knowledge, and integrate them into a single business-intelligence platform.

- Measure experiences with and across all types of touchpoints.

- Gather structured and unstructured customer perception data, as expressed to your company and across the Internet.

- Make customer insight data available across your company.

Benefits your organization may expect:

- The ability to intelligently respond to customer needs with personalized products, services, touchpoints, and experiences.

- Automated customer interactions through smart touchpoints.

- Aligned and seamless customer experiences, delivered consistently across all channels and customer segments.

- To leverage customer data as a strategic asset to improve operations and drive customer engagement.

REWARD YOUR EMPLOYEES FOR WIN/WIN BEHAVIORS

It's not possible for a company to act smart unless its employees are motivated and enabled to do so.

Rewarding your employees for finding ways that both your customers and company profit from – and giving them the tools to do so – is a critical element in keeping up with the needs of your smart customers.

In most companies, employees aren't clear on which customers drive value, what touchpoints and experiences are most important to them, or what their roles and responsibilities are when it comes to delivering better customer experiences.

This is a problem. For a company to act smart, it needs to:

- Reward employees for serving the needs of its most valuable customers;

- Enable employees to better serve customers through easy access to accurate data;

- Reasonably empower employees to improve experiences;

- Reward employees for designing and utilizing modular products, services, and processes.

When a company enables and rewards employees in these ways, customers will notice the difference. Such actions enable a firm's ability to leverage areas of strength and minimize areas of weakness, while becoming more responsive and more flexible in the face of change.

RESPONSIVENESS + FLEXIBILITY = FORMULA FOR GROWTH

Most efforts to change corporate performance are so complicated they are doomed to fail from day one. Here's the opposite, two simple and straightforward changes in your reward system: Build your share of each customer's business, and create modular capabilities. Institute them, and your company will become more customer-centric and responsive to customer needs.

Smart companies respond in meaningful ways.

In many traditional firms, most customer feedback is ignored. But a firm that's organized around the needs of its most valuable customers is able to respond to feedback in a variety of ways. When a customer says, "I wish this was different," you can make it different by improving the experience for that customer at that moment, and by improving the experience for all – if the data dictates.

Drive value by structuring employee rewards around the needs of your most valuable customers.

No longer just ask, "Did we generate more revenue this year than last?" Now, you must also ask, "Did we increase the value of each of our most valuable customers this year, compared to last? And did we increase the value of them all?" Problems that had been masked through acquisition of new customers will become visible, and can be fixed.

In such an organization, change and adaptation is natural; it happens daily, one person at a time. Contrast this with traditionally product-driven firms, where change can be wrenching because it happens so rarely.

The changes we're talking about have just begun to occur. But most companies don't see this, and won't until it's too late. Unless your employees are empowered and rewarded to help in these ways, your firm will have change forced upon it.

Questions to ask:

- Have you (reasonably) empowered your employees to solve customer problems and to improve customer experiences?

- Does your onboarding process help new hires understand their role in serving customers?

- Are your reward structures in alignment with the needs and desired actions of your most valuable customers?

Steps you can take:

- Create crystal-clear profiles of your most valuable customers and their needs, and share these across your company.

- Ensure that your brand – and the customer experience that it promises – is clearly articulated and understood by all.

- Give your employees the tools they need to better serve your customers – including authority and access to data.

- Reward (compensate and promote) your employees for acting smart, and for serving the needs of your customers.

- Focus on ALL employees; not just customer-facing ones.

Benefits your organization may expect:

- Your firm will adapt more quickly and be more responsive to changing customer needs and rapidly evolving markets.

- Customer experience will improve, helping to increase loyalty.

- Employee loyalty will improve, strengthening customer service.

TRANSFORM TOUCHPOINTS (AND MAKE THEM SMART)

Transform your touchpoints to better meet customer needs, and make them smart enough to do so even more effectively.

We've already discussed that touchpoints are all the places your company touches its customers: products, packaging, stores, support, website, call center, ads, emails, etc.

A dumb touchpoint is inflexible, unchanging. Think of a print advertisement or a flyer. A smart touchpoint is one that can sense what a customer does and respond appropriately. It can gather data, which means it enables your firm to learn.

Transforming touchpoints – and finding opportunities to make them smarter – is what allows any company to get smart about their customers, and serve them more intelligently as a result. To unlock the power of touchpoints, your company needs to:

- Understand the importance and effectiveness of touchpoints;

- Based on this knowledge, look for opportunities to innovate customer experience (vs. focusing on innovating products) by customizing touchpoints to better meet customer needs;

- Make dumb touchpoints smart by adding intelligence (such as sensing and responding to customer needs, or gathering data).

Too many companies consider touchpoints from a silo perspective. Call centers have phone-based human touchpoints. Marketing creates touchpoints to sell something, or perform a basic marketing function. You get the idea. But touchpoints have the ability to be dramatically more powerful than this.

TOUCHPOINTS ARE INCREASINGLY DIGITAL ("SMART")

Smart touchpoints are at the heart of delivering smarter customer experiences. The smarter your touchpoints, the stronger the digital relationships they help you build, the more (and more relevant) the data you can gather and the more intelligent you and your company will become. Not embracing smart touchpoints? Kind of stupid.

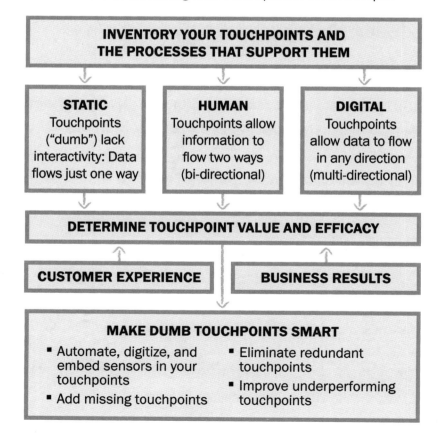

Smart touchpoints deliver personalized experiences while simultaneously making you smarter about your customers.

Customized services are the foundation of innovative customer experience. In our app-driven, always-connected world, "one size fits all" doesn't fly anymore. And it doesn't have to.

Bringing digital innovation and smart touchpoints into the mix lets companies modularize services in ways that are totally replicable, yet completely customized. Think iTunes, Netflix, or Pandora. Or consider Zipcar. As a customer, your experience is totally personalized, based on where you are and what you want. Zipcar brings offline processes online, helping you find and choose the best car for you, no matter where you are.

They also use this data to help them improve experience and drive value, giving them about double the revenue and efficiency of a traditional car rental company. Mass customization driven by smart touchpoints creates highly personal experiences that are difficult for competitors to match.

Smart touchpoints make it possible to monitor what happens when customers use your services. For example, Sage Software has downloaded over a billion data points from its customers' daily usage of its products, and uses this information to help customers understand how to better leverage their software.[1] It also uses this data to intelligently upsell products and services.

Smart touchpoints open up all sorts of opportunities.

Questions to ask:

- Where can smart touchpoints help you better understand customer needs – and provide better experiences?

- Where can dumb touchpoints be improved by making them smart? Or can they be eliminated, if not that important?

- How can smart touchpoints drive "mass customization," personalizing experiences and products for your customers?

- Can you bring offline processes online?

Steps you can take:

- Map your customer journey to see where needs can be better met and experience improved by smart touchpoints.

- Map your touchpoints to learn which are most important, and to see if the right touchpoints are in the right places.

- Map your systems for touchpoint management and delivery so you can reduce cost, and increase efficiencies.

Benefits your organization may expect:

- Improved customer experience, because the touchpoints customers encounter will be tailored to their needs.

- The ability to see into the future by analyzing the data that smart touchpoints generate from customer interactions.

- Reduced costs and increased efficiencies, as dumb and redundant touchpoints are removed or modified.

IN SUMMARY: IT REALLY PAYS TO GET – AND ACT – SMART

The framework we present in this chapter provides a way for organizations of all sizes and kinds to better serve their customers, and increase margins and revenue in the process.

At its core, however, acting "smart" is a way to leverage technology and innovation in new ways to do something the best companies have always done better than their competition: Give customers what they want.

It's as simple as this: Listen to your customers. Respond to their needs – even those they don't yet know they have. And make this a priority for your team.

Ivy League Education, Online? Stanford University is as good as it gets. Now you can take many of their courses for free, via iTunes. It may not be as good as attending Stanford and hanging out in the courtyard, but it's a lot better than paying for a bad course elsewhere. In many ways it's getting easier to keep up with the pace of innovation – if you have the initiative.

KEY TAKEAWAYS:

- Segment customers by needs, and your company will have an easier time setting priorities and making investment decisions.

- Modularize your capabilities, to make your company more nimble and better able to adapt to changing customer needs.

- Anticipate customer needs by recognizing patterns and responding in a manner that saves customers time, money, and effort.

- Reward employees for win/win behaviors and embracing this SMART approach to business.

- Transform your touchpoints to better meet customer needs, and give each the ability to sense and respond, so your products and company can act smart.

Six:
Critical
Steps

"IF ANYONE DISRUPTS THIS INDUSTRY, IT'S GOING TO BE US."

Massive disruption is coming, and the only question is whether your firm is going to cause it or fall victim to it. Disruption is not easy, either to create or to confront.

We have no illusions about that.

But in the spirit of helping established firms best serve their customers, we offer 10 ways your firm could disrupt its own industry, raising the standards of customer experience and creating new opportunities for growth:

1. Build wireless sensors into your products.

2. Totally eliminate your industry's persistent customer pain points.

3. Dramatically reduce complexity.

4. Cut prices 90 percent (or more).

5. Make stupid objects smart.

6. Teach your company to talk.

7. Be utterly transparent.

8. Let customers make or assemble their own products.

9. Make loyalty dramatically easier than disloyalty.

10. Sell an ongoing service, not just a product.

Let's take a look at each possibility...

1) Build wireless sensors into your products.

If this possibility isn't obvious already, then we haven't made the case about digital sensors as a disruptive force. Sensors make dumb products smart, gathering information from the environment that you can use to gain competitive advantage and to better serve your customers.

Through sensors you can learn how customers actually use your products, and guide them in gaining greater benefits from them. For example, instead of just building a thermostat to control the heat in a building, you could add additional sensors to determine the way air circulates through the building and identify energy inefficiencies.

Sensors can detect minor problems in your products before they become major problems, and allow you to fix a problem before your customer is even aware of it. This could reduce your average response time for a problem from four hours down to immediately.

Sensors can create additional revenue streams from existing products. An appliance company could add weight sensors in a refrigerator and create a new business automatically replenishing food items as soon as they run low. A B2B manufacturer could install sensors in its distributors' warehouses and do the same.

2) Totally eliminate your industry's persistent customer pain points.

Each industry has practices that drive customers crazy.

Technology providers drive customers crazy with technical support that requires long waits on hold and hopelessly complex interactions ("Just find the serial number on the back of your device and type that into the space provided along with your IP address and the exact wording of the error message you encountered").

Credit card issuers (and telecom providers, cable companies, etc.) require callers to provide their account number multiple times in different ways, then answer a series of questions to positively identify themselves.

Unsurprisingly, these are the exact types of practices that cause customers to believe a company is behaving stupidly.

What practices exist in your industry that drive customers crazy? How do all companies in your industry behave stupidly? Identify these types of practices, and wipe them out.

Think: Can we turn our process or perspective around, to look through the customer's eyes as though they were the company and we were the customers?

CHALLENGE: DISRUPT CUSTOMER SERVICE IN YOUR INDUSTRY

What if you could set a new standard for customer experience in your industry? While the tools to do so now exist, you need to ask the right questions to help point the way. These are just a few that you could ask:

"How can we leverage any or each of the disruptive forces described in this book to change this situation?"

- Social Influence
- Digital Sensors
- Pervasive Memory
- Physical Web

"If we had no infrastructure, no politics, no barriers, and no limitations – how would we exploit our own limitations?"

"How do we save our customers, time, money, and effort?"

"How do we better serve the needs of our most valuable customers?" (Disruptive technologies push all firms towards serving each customer precisely as they wish to be served.)

Let's pretend that customer service is the major pain point in your industry. How do you fix it by looking at things from your customers' perspective? For example, why can't they put your firm on hold or make you (the company) navigate their voicemail system? Such questions may seem silly at first, but these disruptive technologies are literally turning many situations upside-down.

HOW DRAMATICALLY CAN WE REDUCE OR ELIMINATE THE TIME IT TAKES CUSTOMERS TO INTERACT WITH CUSTOMER SERVICE?

What if ...

- Customers booked time through an online calendar, and reps contacted the customer at the scheduled time?

- When customers opted to leave a message rather than wait on hold, they could choose a specific call back time (and actually get called back)?

- You connected each product customers used to an analytical service at the company, so that reps could more quickly diagnose problems and offer customers relevant guidance?

- Using such a service, you solved customer problems remotely, minimizing or eliminating the need for a call? Even better, you solved problems before customers were aware of them.

- You could eliminate data silos, so that all customer information is instantly accessible to any rep?

- Ratings and specialties of specific service reps were posted online, allowing customers to choose (and rate) who serves them? What if rep compensation was tied to these ratings?

- Voicemail trees were posted online, and you allowed customers to click at a specific point in the tree to initiate the call, thus skipping the entire navigation process?

Of course this list could be much longer, but this gives you the basic idea. Now that you have a starting point and a roadmap, where can you disrupt your industry?

3) Dramatically reduce complexity.

A company we have been tracking for some time – Simple, formerly known as BankSimple – is trying to take a machete to the insanely complex and confusing world of consumer banking. Recognizing that banks do a pretty good job of managing money but a poor job of managing customers, Simple has been designing vastly simpler customer interfaces and tools.

Simple plans to partner with, not compete against, established banks. They'll manage the customers while their banking partners manage the money.

Similarly, you might decide to partner with one or more upstart firms so that they can simplify the tasks that you do poorly, while your firm retains control over its core competencies.

Zipcar simplified the car rental process by allowing customers to simply unlock and drive any Zipcar they come across: no quotes, no rental counters, no paperwork, no lines.

Services such as EZPass simplified going through toll booths.

The more complex the processes and practices in your industry, the greater your opportunity to gain competitive advantage by simplifying them.

Yes, doing so will be very hard. But that's the whole point; the first firm to do so gains tremendous advantages.

4) Cut prices 90 percent (or more).

Incremental change doesn't disrupt an industry; radical change does. The disruptive forces outlined in this book will create numerous opportunities to radically change the costs of serving customers.

We suggested building wireless sensors into your products and pointed out how doing so could allow you to prevent problems before they occurred. In some industries – such as construction or manufacturing – this sort of preventative monitoring could reduce service downtime costs by a factor of 10 or more.

Radical price reductions require radical new processes and business models. Smartphones and tablets create numerous opportunities to identify these. Recently we replaced a $500 marine navigation unit with a $20 iPad app that works better. Our phones eliminate the need for a watch or calculator.

You don't cut prices by 90 percent through marginal improvements in existing products. You do it by asking, "What problem are we trying to solve for the customer, and how do these disruptive forces create opportunities for us to solve it in a far more efficient manner?"

TRANSMIT   GEOLOCATE   SHARE

5) Make stupid objects smart.

We didn't think this one up. The race is on to make everything smart, and the dumber your products were to begin with, the greater the opportunity to make them smart.

Think of a garbage dumpster that calls central dispatch when it is full, eliminating the need for the customer to do so or your office to send out a driver. That same dumpster could warn the customer when it is overweight, and point out that it would be cheaper to empty it now than to further overfill it.

No offense to dogs, but their collars could alert owners when the dog wanders away, barks excessively, or jumps on the furniture.

Light bulbs could flash before they burn out. Baseballs could announce how fast they were thrown. Plants could politely request water when they are too dry, or shout out when you try to overwater them.

Oil and propane tanks should call for refill when they reach a level the customer specifies. Doors should be able to text message you when they open (so you know your son is home from school).

Take every product you sell, and make it smart...or accept the fact that you must forevermore compete on price and accept low margins.

WIRELESS

24 HR. SERVICE

SMARTPHONE

SEEN A GOOD NOUN LATELY?

The Noun Project (www.thenounproject.com) "collects, organizes, and adds to the highly recognizable symbols that form the world's visual language, so we may share them in a fun and meaningful way."

In other words, it's a free collection of symbols, the best we've seen anywhere. And it's growing, fast.

Anyone can now submit symbols to the project, as long as they accept the free-to-all approach, and they can design a symbol that is simple and very easy to recognize.

Similarly, more than 100 million photos and illustrations by amateur photographers and artists – many whose work is better than that of professionals – are available through a creative commons license for businesses and individuals to use.[1]

While the business of stock photography and illustration hasn't disappeared, it has certainly changed.

The common thread? Those who provide symbols to The Noun Project or photos through Flickr are driven by a desire to create, and to contribute. And their numbers are growing while their interests spread to other areas.

It is very hard to compete with people who are more driven by quality than money, and whose numbers grows every day. Far better to support, encourage, and nurture such folks.

6) Teach your company to talk.

Apple recently introduced the Siri personal assistant on the iPhone; "she" allows you to have a conversation with your phone. Your iPhone can now access the Internet as well as the information it stores, both understanding and responding appropriately to your statements.

Flash-forward two to five years from now. What if your company could talk to customers? We don't mean that your employees talk on behalf on the company. We mean that a digital, computerized persona speaks on behalf of your firm.

It takes orders. It provides support. It answers questions. It upsells. It issues refunds. All of this, and more, in response to verbal requests by customers.

The toughest part of this challenge is not technical, although a few problems still need to be solved.

The tough part is knocking down the walls that separate your databases and departments. It's deciding whose product gets cross-sold, who gets "credit" for sales, and who "owns" the customer.

Our view is simple. No one owns the customer, and you either do what's best for the customer or you will lose him. But the real question we want to put forward is this: what happens if your competitors' companies talk, but yours doesn't?

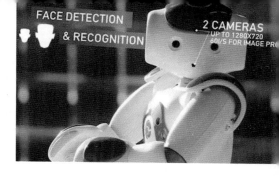

Aldebaran Robotics' sensor-packed NAO robot walks and talks, recognizes people and their voices, and understands the intent of spoken requests. (So, how well does your IVR system work again?)

What will happen when you try to transfer customers from customer service to credit and then back to customer service again? How many will hang up? More importantly, how many will leave, never to return?

If your company could talk, you could:

- Provide true one-stop shopping;

- Duplicate (then modularize and integrate) the best practices of top sales and support personnel;

- Combine a great sales person with a great service person, two qualities seldom found in the same human;

- Answer any question accurately, assuming the correct answer is in the database;

- Connect to sensors spread around your company or the world, changing prices, offers, and terms based on the latest market conditions;

- Remove significant amounts of friction from customer relationships;

- Eliminate the need to transfer customers from one department to another.

EteRNA is an example of citizen involvement in cutting-edge scientific research.
Developed by scientists at Carnegie Mellon and Stanford universities, this online game challenges players to discover new ways to fold RNA molecules. Common wisdom would have said you can't use non-scientists to conduct research; in truth, you can.

The *New York Times* reported, "EteRNA is a successor to Foldit, a popular Internet video game that proved that the pattern matching skills of amateurs could outperform some of the best protein-folding algorithms designed by scientists."[2]

7) Be utterly transparent.

Think: No secrets, and no spin.

We've described how Social Influence and Pervasive Memory will make it increasingly difficult for companies to hide from dissatisfied customers, negative reviews and faulty products.

What if your company didn't simply try to stop hiding, but instead radically embraced the truth? How might it impact your culture to decide that your firm would be the most powerful force in your industry making certain that every spec of the truth was obvious to every customer, analyst, and reviewer? Would it change your reward systems? Would it impact employee motivation? Might it cause changes in the kind of employees you attract and retain?

We're pretty opinionated in this regard. The truth is coming, and there's nothing you can do about it. But most firms won't recognize this until it happens. Better to get far out in front while confusion reigns.

8) Let customers make or assemble their own products.

The disruptive forces we've profiled push each industry closer to personalization, because tailoring services for customers is just part of acting smart. The closer you move production to a customer, the greater the opportunities to personalize.

Lego toys have often been used as an example when explaining mass customization, since standard pieces can be combined in unique ways to create unique products. But even Lego realized some years ago that it could allow customers to design their own products online, then have the necessary piece shipped to them. The more modular you make the pieces that combine to create your products, the greater your ability to allow customers to combine individual parts in unique ways.

There's a whole spectrum of possibilities. You can manufacture a product yourself, and then allow the customer to superficially customize it. You can make a product and design it so that customers customize it in a substantial manner; this describes perfectly how customers install apps on smartphones, tablets, and computers. The challenge is to conceive of ways to leapfrog your competitors and generally accepted industry standards.

At the same time, technologies such as 3D printing raise the increasingly real possibility of locating mini "manufacturing plants" at the customer's location. You could literally have your customers make the entire product.

IN-HOME MANUFACTURING?

For under $500, the Printrbot 3D printer has the ability to manufacture parts up to 1 square foot in size, almost anywhere. In fact, since many of the parts are plastic, Printrbot is coming close to being a self-repl icating machine.

Such printers melt a plastic similar to that used in Lego pieces, and create a replacement part or original design. The resulting piece can be highly complex, and very durable.

Yes, people use these at home. And they're certain to get cheaper and better. As more competitors enter the market, we won't be surprised when 3D printer prices drop to what paper printers cost. (Remember how much early laser printers were?)

Michael Dell forever changed the personal computer business by offering customer-configured PCs, delivered to your home or office, ready to run. 3D printers are potentially much more disruptive, offering even greater opportunities.

What if your company never had to actually make, store, or ship physical products?

Meet Your MakerBot.
From chess sets and toy robots to small-scale industrial products and replacement parts, users dream up new applications daily. It's no wonder that MakerBot Industries is selling Replicators as fast as they can make them.

> **"YOU'VE GOT TO LOOK FOR A GAP, WHERE COMPETITORS HAVE GROWN LAZY AND LOST CONTACT WITH THE CUSTOMER."**
> — RUPERT MURDOCH, CHAIRMAN AND CEO OF NEWS CORPORATION

9) Make loyalty dramatically easier than disloyalty.

According to Don Clark writing in his *Wall Street Journal* blog, Intel executive Mooly Eden once asked an audience how many had cell phones, and then how many were married.

Then, he asked if any of the married people would be willing to hand over their phone if their spouse lost his or hers. None would. "That is my point," said Eden. "That is personalization."[3]

By definition, when companies act smart they are personalizing the way they interact with and serve customers. Once you start delivering personalization, you create immense opportunities to make loyalty more convenient than disloyalty.

- You can store customer preferences, and act on them.
- You can save the customer time, money, and effort – especially by eliminating repetitive tasks.
- You can provide auto-replenishment of needed supplies.
- You can monitor products remotely, and service them before they break instead of afterwards.

Think about every major purchase decision your customers face in your industry. How can you make it easier for customers to remain with your firm? Now, think even bigger. Can it be five or ten times easier? Subtlety can be lost on today's customers.

The challenge is to make loyalty so much more convenient, so radically easy, that customers won't even consider switching to a competitor. Ever.

10) Sell an ongoing service, not just a product.

In recent years, printer companies shifted their focus from selling printers to selling ink. But most customers still have to remember to buy more ink. What if printer companies sold printers that never ran out of ink, and charged on a per page basis?

Our not-so-secret wish is for a smartphone service that sells guaranteed phone service, rather than a phone that stops working eight months before your contract expires or the phone is "eligible for upgrade."

Many people would gladly pay 30 cents a mile for car transportation, rather than have to buy a car for $35,000.

From your company's viewpoint, selling a service locks in an ongoing relationship and revenue stream. In many industries, the manufacturer has no relationship with the end user and simply makes a sale every few years, at best.

This is an extremely vulnerable position in which to be, and turning products into ongoing services may offer significant benefit not only for your customers but also for your firm.

DISRUPTIVE INNOVATION OCCURS OUTSIDE ESTABLISHED CHANNELS, BUT IS RELENTLESS IN ITS MOVEMENT INTO MARKETS.

At Noisebridge, a 5,600-square-foot collaborative "hacker space" in San Francisco, people with diverse skills, interests and motivations come together to innovate. They're not college friends or business partners. They don't work in the same company. They are just random folks interested in new ideas and technologies.

Duncan Logan, CEO of technology-startup accelerator RocketSpace, has room for about 100 companies in his four-story, Fremont Street building. Applicants need to be seed-funded and have a disruptive business idea. But with up to three new applicants a day, selectivity ratios compete with Ivy League undergraduate admissions – and with good reason. Companies that are accepted get near-instant access to top-tier capital, Silicon Valley connections, and the brightest talent.

Technology incubator programs like Techstars and Y-Combinator (which graduated AirBnB and DropBox) turn teams and their ideas into companies.

Even earlier stage ideas can get a launch pad through groups like Startup Weekend, which brings business and technical teams, mentors, and ideas together in an intensive 54-hour workshop. Since its founding in mid-2007, over 25,000 alumni have "graduated" from Startup Weekends across more than 100 cities in 30 countries.[4]

If you think innovation is something that mainly takes place within established companies, think again.

WELCOME TO SIMULTANEOUS CHANGE

One of the biggest challenges in looking forward two, five, or more years into the future is that everything changes at the same time, not just the elements on which you are presently focused. Social media experts think social media will change everything. App developers think apps will change everything. But in reality, everything is changing at once.

Here's the safest prediction we can make: Everything will get smarter.

Where you go next depends on your industry and your company. If you wish to compete on price and sell low-quality commodity products, then you can safely ignore much of what we have said. If you wish to maintain your margins and be a market leader, you will need to act smart, to leverage sensors, to support the emerging Physical Web, and to develop a strategy for interacting with customers while they simultaneously interact with everyone else.

You will need to replace your dumb touchpoints with smart ones. You will need to become obsessed with saving your customers time, money, and effort. You will need to provide customized services. You will need to do all these things, most likely in a radically different way.

Most importantly, you will need to focus with laser-like intensity on the intersection of initiatives that benefit your customers and benefit your firm.

To that end, we offer a simple chart that summarizes immense opportunities. It compares the four disruptive forces to four potential benefits your business could deliver to specific customer segments.

Each blank box represents one or more opportunities. Don't be limited by the size of the boxes; this chart just gives you the basic idea. Some of those boxes represent opportunities capable of producing millions of dollars in new revenues.

BENEFITS TO CUSTOMERS THAT ARE NOW POSSIBLE

	Save Time	Save Money	Reduce Effort	Customize Services
Social Influence inserts others between companies and customers				
Pervasive Memory generates data from every digital interaction				
Digital Sensors transforms *everything* from dumb to smart				
Physical Web brings the Web's habits and capabilities to the real world				

Each of the four disruptive forces has the ability to create massive benefits for your customers, as well as for your company. We've outlined four of the most obvious, each with the potential to create significant opportunity.

BE SMART ENOUGH TO LEARN WHAT YOUR CUSTOMERS REALLY NEED

In the last chapter, we spoke about the importance of segmenting customers by their needs. Doing so enables your business to escape the trap of speaking generically about customer needs.

All your customers are not the same.

Starting with specific, needs-based segments, you must get even more detailed about the capabilities, products, and services your company must offer each segment.

Do not base this list on management hunches. Interact with people. Watch customers make actual – not simulated – purchase decisions, or not.

STOP.

Let's get real. Many of you aren't going to do this. You don't have a culture that puts customers first. You'd rather sell than serve. You might be flush with your own success, or reacting to changing marketplace realities that "go beyond" customer needs.

One word: Netflix.

Even the biggest success stories can lose focus on customer needs. Netflix ran hugely successful competitions to challenge developers to make their movie recommendation service even more personal.

**"... INNOVATION RARELY MAKES ITS WAY BY GRADUALLY
WINNING OVER AND CONVERTING ITS OPPONENTS: WHAT DOES
HAPPEN IS THAT THE OPPONENTS GRADUALLY DIE OUT."**

— MAX PLANCK, PHYSICIST

They not only understood the absolute importance of getting highly granular about what individual customers need (What should I watch tonight?), but they also set higher standards for themselves than any other firm in their industry. They disrupted the industry leader, Blockbuster.

Then they forgot it all and decided to split their services into two pieces, and to force customers to duplicate their preferences into two parallel but independent recommendation engines. Customers revolted, and did so in huge numbers over a relatively low price point. Management was humiliated, and had to back down.

And Netflix is among the best.

Not only does technology force companies to get increasingly granular about customer needs – and to become obsessive in this regard – it also gives companies the ability to do so.

But the odds are your firm does not understand this yet. That's why we wrote this book. Good people work for your firm. Your team has children who depend on you. We'd much rather see established firms anticipate and successfully meet changing customer expectations than to fall victim to complacency and lack of focus.

Obsession is not always pretty to watch, but your business really needs to obsess over the specific needs of specific customers.

And while you're doing it, try this...

ONCE YOUR FIRM COMMITS TO ACTING
SMARTER, YOU WILL SEE THAT THE
POSSIBILITIES ARE ENDLESS. THERE'S A
RACE TO GET SMART; AND IF YOU'RE NOT
IN IT, YOU CANNOT WIN IT.

START MAKING YOUR COMPANY SMARTER, NOW

"Do or do not. There is no try," exhorts Yoda as Luke Skywalker complains his task is impossible, but he will try anyway.

It is not impossible for a company to act smart. Many firms do this already, and with each week smart firms are leapfrogging each other.

It is not impossible to create, say, a Talking Company, even if this means cleaning all the junk out of your databases, changing job descriptions, revising the metrics around which your team gets paid, and developing a business model that supports such an initiative.

It is, however, very hard. It requires intense focus. It may not make sense for your firm.

We fully understand that many of you work for companies that are so far away from acting smart it keeps you up at night. If this is the case with you, and you don't own the company, you might consider looking for another job.

But let's assume you decide to stay.

Here's what we know for certain: our theory about everything getting smarter? It's no theory. It's happening now.

Start now.

Hard as we have labored over these words, it's action that matters, not words.

We hope you will visit us online at smartcustomers.com. Our goal is to start a conversation around what it will take to profitably serve smart customers. We welcome not only your feedback to the book, but also your personal observations regarding the specific challenges, opportunities, and success stories you encounter.

If you want personal attention, we are happy to provide that as well. We would love to help your firm leapfrog its competitors and delight its customers.

Michael Hinshaw
San Francisco, California
michael@smartcustomers.com

Bruce Kasanoff
Westport, Connecticut
bruce@smartcustomers.com

KEY TAKEAWAYS:

- Be the first established firm to disrupt your own industry, because it's going to happen anyway and it's more profitable (and fun) to be the disruptor than the victim of disruption.

- Eliminate common problems and hassles that drive customers crazy.

- Use the four disruptive forces to drive innovation and include people from outside your firm when doing so.

- Make it dramatically more convenient for customers to be loyal than disloyal.

- The race is on to make everything smart. It has already started.

Authors

ACKNOWLEDGEMENTS

Our first acknowledgement is to you, for investing time and effort in this book.

As writers and strategists, we're continually thrilled when our insights inspire change and innovation. We hope that this book will spark your ideas and insights as well.

For Michael, particular gratitude is due to my wife, Cameron, and my children, William and Julia, all of whom both encouraged me and put up with my distraction as this book was created.

For Bruce, great thanks to Kate for your patience over the long stretches required to bring this book to fruition, and to Alyssa, Jeff and Matt for inspiring me with your own achievements.

Special thanks go to the three Denises: Denise della Santina for early criticism and ongoing sage advice; Denise Marshall, for her research and sourcing skills, and Denise Szott, whose skill as a production designer and manager ensured that what you hold in your hand looks as we intended. Thanks also to Lisa Hamilton for proofing and editing, and Lannette Ingels and Kris Clark for coordination and overall project management.

We have been energized by the wide group of friends and business associates who both encouraged and exhorted us to follow this path. We'll be thanking you personally, because you are the fuel that made this happen.

MICHAEL HINSHAW

A successful entrepreneur, executive and teacher, Michael Hinshaw has spent his career integrating creativity and business strategy to improve how companies think about, connect with, and serve their customers.

His unique blend of strategic thinking and design innovation helps companies – from fast-growth market leaders to the Fortune 100 – drive significant value by transforming customer interactions and the processes that support them.

Michael has advised global organizations including Argo Group, Danone, McKesson, T. Rowe Price, and the United Methodist Church on brand, customer experience and loyalty, translating business strategies into distinctive brands, products, services, and experiences.

Currently President of Touchpoint Metrics and Managing Director of MCorp Consulting, Michael previously served as President and CEO of Verida – a public company with operations throughout North America – where he grew the company from inception to a $300 million business.

Today, Michael helps companies leverage disruption to stay ahead of the rapidly changing needs of their customers. He earned his MFA in Design from the Academy of Art University. Michael is also a mentor and guest lecturer on entrepreneurship at U.C. Berkeley's Haas School of Business.

BRUCE KASANOFF

Bruce Kasanoff focuses on marketing and innovation, the two areas that drive revenue growth. He blogs about each at NowPossible.com.

He works with both leading companies and aggressive growth firms across a wide range of industries. He also delivers workshops and speeches on customer experience, personalization, and innovation. An entrepreneur as well, Bruce has raised about $20 million in venture capital and built sales of a new product line from zero to $20 million in three years.

The Chartered Institute of Marketing – the largest organization of marketing professionals in the world – cited Bruce among its inaugural listing of the 50 most influential thinkers in marketing and business today.

As an original partner at the 1to1 marketing consultancy, Peppers & Rogers Group, he helped grow that firm from 10 to 150 employees in three years.

Bruce is the author of *Making It Personal: How to Profit from Personalization without Invading Privacy,* a critically acclaimed book that predicted many of the innovations we see today.

He earned an MBA from The Wharton School and has presented at Yale, NYU, Wharton, and Babson College.

Index

Sources

QUOTES:

Page vii

Shinseki, E. K. 2002. "Deputy Secretary Wolfowitz Interview with The New Yorker." US Department of Defense. June 18. Retrieved January 18, 2012. http://www.defenselink.mil/transcripts/transcript.aspx?transcriptid=3527

INTRODUCTION

IMAGES:

Page 6

©2006 Rocket Raccoon

SECTION 1

1. Bustillo, Miguel and Ann Zimmerman. 2010. "Phone-Wielding Shoppers Strike Fear Into Retailers." *Wall Street Journal*. December 1.
2. Perez, Sarah. 2011. "Sunday Is The Best Day To Launch Your Mobile App." TechCrunch. December 19. Retrieved January 18, 2012. http://techcrunch.com/2011/12/19/sunday-is-the-best-day-to-launch-your-mobile-app/
3. Ogg, Erica. 2011. "What happens when the iPad outsells the Mac." CNET. January 24. Retrieved January 17, 2012. http://news.cnet.com/8301-31021_3-20029258-260.html#ixzz1DO1GZJco
4. Tsukayama, Hayley. 2011. "Apple's Record iPad Sales, In Context." Washington Post. January 24.
5. mobiThinking. 2012. "Global mobile statistics 2012: all quality mobile marketing research, mobile Web stats, subscribers, ad revenue, usage, trends..." February. Retrieved April 1, 2012. http://mobithinking.com/mobile-marketing-tools/latest-mobile-stats
6. Socialistic. 2011. "Big Changes In Holiday Retail." December 8. Retrieved January 18, 2012. http://www.socialistic.com/2011/12/big-changes-in-holiday-retail/
7. Online Marketing Trends. 2011. "Retail Shopping via Mobile : Apps vs Mobile Platforms." November 30. Retrieved January 18, 2012. http://www.onlinemarketing-trends.com/2011/11/retail-shopping-via-mobile-apps-vs.html
8. NielsenWire. 2011. "Cellphones and Global Youth: Mobile Internet and Messaging Trends." January 11. Retrieved January 18, 2012. http://blog.nielsen.com/nielsenwire/online_mobile/cellphones-and-global-youth-mobile-internet-and-messaging-trends/
9. Chetan, Sharma. 2011. "US Mobile Data Market Update Q4 2010 and 2010." February 28. Retrieved January 18, 2012. http://www.chetansharma.com/blog/2011/02/28/us-mobile-data-market-update-q4-2010-and-2010/
10. Cisco. 2011. "Cisco Visual Networking Index: Global Mobile Data Traffic Forecast Update, 2010–2015." February 1. Retrieved January 18, 2012. http://www.cisco.com/en/US/solutions/collateral/ns341/ns525/ns537/ns705/ns827/white_paper_c11-520862.html
11. BusinessWire. 2011. "55 Percent of Retailers Cite Shoppers as Better Connected To Information than Store Associates, According To Motorola Solutions Survey." January 10. Retrieved January 18, 2012. http://www.businesswire.com/news/home/20110110005368/en/55-Percent-Retailers-Cite-Shoppers-Connected-Information
12. ibid.
13. Hsieh, Tony. 2010. Delivering Happiness: A Path to Profits, Passion, and Purpose. New York: Grand Central.

QUOTES:
Page 11

Pine II, Joseph, et al. 2011. *Infinite Possibility: Creating Customer Value on the Digital Frontier.* San Francisco: Berrett-Koehler.

Page 13

Gates, Bill. 1999. *Business at the Speed of Thought: Using a Digital Nervous System.* New York: Warner.

Page 17

Kamen, Dean. (n.d.) Retrieved March 30, 2012. http://www.brainyquote.com/quotes/authors/d/dean_kamen.html

Page 21

Seidman, Dov. 2007. *How: Why How We Do Anything Means Everything.* Hoboken: Wiley

Page 27

Halligan, Brian, and Dharmesh Shah. 2010. Inbound Marketing: Get Found Using Google, Social Media, and Blogs. Hoboken: Wiley.

Page 31

Kennedy, John F. June 25, 1963. "Address in the Assembly Hall at Paulskirche." Frankfurt, Germany.

IMAGES:

Page 18-19

©2010 Cait Sith

Page 25

Courtesy of Patricia A. Minicucci

Page 30

©2010 Michael Kappel

SECTION 2

1. Hopkins, Brian. 2011. "Big Data Will Help Shape Your Market's Next Big Winners." Forrester: *Brian Hopkins' Blog.* September 30. Retrieved January 18, 2012. http://blogs.forrester.com/brian_hopkins/11-09-30-big_data_will_help_shape_your_markets_next_big_winners

2. Evans, Bob. 2011. "Global CIO: IBM's Most Disruptive Acquisition Of 2010 Is Netezza." *InformationWeek.* February 7. Retrieved January 18, 2012. http://www.informationweek.com/news/global-cio/interviews/229201238

3. Zeal Optics. Retrieved January 18, 2012. http://www.zealoptics.com/transcend-2.html

QUOTES:

Page 36

Mature Living. June 1995

Page 40

Miner, Rich. AddictedtoSuccess.com. Retrieved March 10, 2012. http://addicted2success.com

Page 43

Brown, Mark. 2011. "Study Estimates Human Information Capacity at 256 Exabytes." *Wired UK.* February 14. Retrieved January 18, 2012. http://www.wired.co.uk/news/archive/2011-02/14/256-exabytes-of-human-information

Page 49

Negroponte, Nicholas. 1995. *Being Digital.* New York: Random House.

IMAGES:

Page 45

©2011 sellingpix

Page 46

Courtesy of pinktentacle.com

Page 47

Photo of Z3 GPS Goggles courtesy of Zeal Optics

Page 49
    Courtesy of www.autisable.com

SECTION 3
1. Cisco. 2011. "My Shopping, My Way Survey Findings." Retrieved January 18, 2012. http://www.cisco.com/web/about/ac79/docs/retail/Mashop-survey-metrics_UNITED-STATES.pdf
2. Facebook. 2012. "Statistics: People on Facebook". Retrieved March 27, 2012. http://www.facebook.com/press/info.php?statistics
3. ibid.
4. Khaled, Ali. 2011. "Revolution tears down the wall between the internet and us". National. February 9. Retrieved January 18, 2012. http://www.thenational.ae/thenationalconversation/culture-comment/revolution-tears-down-the-wall-between-the-internet-and-us
5. ibid.
6. Hamlin, Kaliya. 2011. "Personal Data Ecosystem talk at Digital Privacy Forum, Jan 20th, 2011 in NYC." Identity Woman. January 20. Retrieved January 18, 2012. http://www.identitywoman.net/personal-data-ecosystem-talk-at-digital-privacy-forum-jan-20th-2011-in-nyc
7. Peckham, Matt. 2011. "iPad Who? Microsoft Talks 8 Million Kinect 'Sold'" PC World. January 6. Retrieved January 18, 2012. http://www.pcworld.com/article/215784/ipad_who_microsoft_talks_8_million_kinect_sold.html
8. Pogue, David. 2010. "Kinect Pushes Users Into a Sweaty New Dimension." New York Times. November 4. Retrieved January 18, 2012. http://www.nytimes.com/2010/11/04/technology/personaltech/04pogue.html?pagewanted=all
9. UBM TechInsights. "Five Trends That Will Shape the Mobile Industry in 2011." Retrieved March 30, 2012. http://www.ubmtechinsights.com/trends/
10. ibid.
11. Sensors. 2012. Retrieved January 19, 2012. http://sensorsmag.globalspec.com/

QUOTES:
Page 59
    Boyd, Danah. AddictedtoSuccess.com. Retrieved March 10, 2012. http://addicted2success.com
Page 67
    Hopkins, Brian. 2011. "Big Data Will Help Shape Your Market's Next Big Winners." Forrester: *Brian Hopkins' Blog*. September 30. Retrieved January 18, 2012. http://blogs.forrester.com/brian_hopkins/11-09-30-big_data_will_help_shape_your_markets_next_big_winners
Page 83
    Berners-Lee, Tim. 18th International World Wide Web Conference (WWW2009). Quoted in D. Silva. 2009. "Internet has only just begun, say founders." PhysOrg. April 22. Retrieved January 18, 2012. http://phys.org/news159644537.html

IMAGES:
Page 55
    ©2009 Luis Argerich
Page 58 and Page 61
    Courtesy of MCorp Consulting
Page 68
    Dan Little Photography, Courtesy of HRL Laboratories, LLC
Page 79
    ©2011 Cosm

SECTION 4

1. Egelhoff, Tom. "Direct Mail: Formula for Success." Small Town Marketing. Retrieved January 18, 2012. http://www.smalltownmarketing.com/direct_mail_formulas.html
2. Gartner, et al. Quoted in Peelen, et al. 2006. "A Study Into the Foundations of CRM Success". NRG Working Paper Series. NRG Working Paper no. 06-09. March.
3. RightNow Technologies. 2010. "Customer Experience Impact Report 2010." October 9. Retrieved January 18, 2012. http://www.slideshare.net/RightNow/2010-customer-experience-impact
4. Quotes are used to make reading easier, but are not direct quotes. They are used to convey the basic intent of what was said.
5. Kestner, John and David Carr. 2011. "Twine: Listen to your world, talk to the Internet" Kickstarter. Retrieved January 18, 2012. http://www.kickstarter.com/projects/supermechanical/twine-listen-to-your-world-talk-to-the-internet
6. ibid.

QUOTES:
Page 91
RightNow Technologies. 2010. "Customer Experience Impact Report 2010". October 9. Retrieved January 18, 2012. http://www.slideshare.net/RightNow/2010-customer-experience-impact

Page 97
Moore, Michael. Quoted in A. Mitchell. 2004. *Beyond Branding: How the New Values of Transparency and Integrity Are Changing the World of Brands.* London: Kogan Page.

Page 110
Young, F. M. (n.d.) FinestQuotes.com. Retrieved March 9, 2012. http://www.finestquotes.com/author_quotes-author-F. M. Young-page-0.htm

Page 115
Welch, Jack. (n.d.) Great-Quotes.com. Retrieved March 9, 2012. http://www.great-quotes.com/quote/801219

IMAGES:
Pages 89
©2006 Christopher Messer
Pages 94-95
Courtesy of The Noun Project
Page 103
Courtesy of Face
Page 106
Courtesy of The Noun Project
Page 112-113
©2012 TedCas
Page 116
©2011 Dwight Eschliman, Courtesy of Nest Labs, Inc.

SECTION 5

1. Jakovljevic, P.J. 2011. "Sage Analyst Day 2011: Not your Older Brother's Sage - Part 3" Technology Evaluation Centers Blog. May 2. Retrieved January 18, 2012. http://blog.technologyevaluation.com/blog/2011/05/02/sage-analyst-day-2011-not-your-older-brother%E2%80%99s-sage-%E2%80%93-part-3/

QUOTES:
Page 125
Peppers, Don and Martha Rogers. 2005. *Return on Customer: Creating Maximum Value From Your Scarcest Resource.* New York: Random House.

Page 129

Sachs, Jeffrey. 2005. *The End of Poverty: Economic Possibilities for Our Time.* New York: Penguin Press.

Page 130

Society for New Communications Research. 2011. "Dell Social Media Listening Command Center (LCC)". Retrieved January 18, 2012. http://sncr.org/node/449

Page 135

Gibson, William. 1995. "Johnny Mnemonic" The Cyberpunk Project. Retrieved January 18, 2012. http://project.cyberpunk.ru/lib/johnny_mnemonic/

IMAGES:

Page 131

©2005 Felix Alim

Page 144

©2009 McSwin

SECTION 6

1. Thorne, Michelle. 2009. "Analysis of 100M CC-Licensed Images on Flickr." Creative Commons. March 25. Retrieved January 18, 2012. http://creativecommons.org/weblog/entry/13588

2. Markoff, John. 2011. "RNA Game Lets Players Help Find a Biological Prize." New York Times. January 10. Retrieved January 18, 2012. http://www.nytimes.com/2011/01/11/science/11rna.html?_r=1

3. Clark, Don. 2009. "Intel Exec Points Up Quirks In the Mobile Market." Wall Street Journal. June 7, Retrieved January 18, 2012. http://blogs.wsj.com/digits/2009/06/07/intel-exec-points-up-quirks-in-the-mobile-market/

4. StartupWeekend.org (2010). "Our Story." Retrieved January 18, 2012. http://startupweekend.org/about/our-story/

IMAGES:

Pages 154-155

Courtesy of The Noun Project

Page 157

Courtesy of Aldebaran Robotics

Page 158

Courtesy of EteRNA

Page 161

Courtesy of MakerBot Industries

Pages 164-165

©2011 Mitch Altman, Cornfield Electronics

Page 171

©2010 Ola Harström

QUOTES:

Page 148

Laing, R.D. (n.d.) BrainyQuote.com. Retrieved March 10, 2012. http://www.brainyquote.com/quotes/authors/r/r_d_laing.html

Page 152

Osborne, Adam. (n.d.) ThinkExist.com. Retrieved March 10, 2012. http://thinkexist.com/quotes/adam_osborne/

Page 162

Murdoch, Rupert. (n.d.) Customer1.com. Retrieved March 10, 2012. http://www.customer1.com/blog/customer-service-quotes

Page 169

Planck, Max. (n.d.) ThinkExist.com. Retrieved March 9, 2012. http://thinkexist.com/quotes/max_planck/

Made in the USA
Lexington, KY
10 October 2012